HAPPY v JOYFUL

Written By:

Frances A. Monroe, FACHE, MHA

Contents

Preface

———— · ★ · ————

Every person carries within them a disposition of whether they are happy or joyful. Though subtle, this distinction is profoundly significant. If we are truly honest with ourselves, most would answer that they are happy. However, what is often labeled as 'happiness' might actually be "fair" or "temporarily pleased with life"—a state of general satisfaction and comfort; yet it does not necessarily equate to the deeper, more enduring state of joy, which I define as blissful contentment.

Human nature often inclines us to mask our true emotions. Society conditions has us to believe that others prefer a sanitized version of our truth, one that avoids disrupting the social fabric with the weight of our real feelings. Thus, when asked, "How are you?", the automatic response is "fine" or "good." These answers are reflexive, devoid of true introspection. We have been taught that revealing our vulnerabilities is a sign of weakness, and so we hide behind these safe, socially acceptable responses.

Happiness often masks a more complex reality. Behind that word may lie unspoken struggles and unvoiced pains. The deeper truths remain buried beneath a veneer of positivity. We wear these masks not just to protect ourselves, but also to shield others from the discomfort of our

-4-

true experiences. It is a delicate dance of maintaining appearances while grappling with the complexities of our inner lives.

As we journey through the highs and lows of human experience in this book, we will explore how joy can be cultivated even in challenging circumstances. This is not just a collection of ideas but a guide to fostering joy in our lives. It encourages introspection, authenticity, and the courage to live our truth, no matter how complex or difficult it may be.

Happiness is fleeting, tied to external circumstances and material comforts. It can be influenced by a sunny day, a promotion at work, or a kind word from a friend. Happiness is wonderful, but it is also temporary and often conditional. Joy, however, is a profound state of being, rooted deeply within our spirit, unshaken by the ebbs and flows of life's blessings or challenges.

Joy is steadfast, a constant presence that persists even in the face of adversity. It is an inner glow that comes from a place of true understanding and acceptance of the beauty of life and what is really important.

The dichotomy of "Happy versus Joyful" is a call to embrace a fuller, richer existence, one where we are not afraid to acknowledge our struggles and celebrate our triumphs. It is about moving beyond the superficial happiness that society often values, and finding a deeper, more resilient joy that can sustain us through the journey of life.

Chapter One

· ★ ·

The Distinct Difference Between Being Happy and Joyful

In the preface, we explored the nuanced distinction between happiness and joyfulness. Happiness, we learned, is often a fleeting state, influenced by external circumstances and material comforts. Joy, on the other hand, is a deeper, more enduring state of being that is rooted within our spirit and remains steadfast through life's blessings and challenges. We set the stage for a deeper understanding of these two states of being.

Understanding these traits is crucial because it allows us to recognize the profound difference between temporary external contentment and enduring internal fulfillment; it allows us to recognize the profound difference between living a life of superficial happiness and embracing a life of true joy. They are perceived positively by those around them, yet their happiness can be transient, easily disrupted by changes in their external environment. Joyful people, however, possess a unique inner radiance (glow) that shines through their eyes, a spring in their step, and an aura of peace that intrigues and sometimes baffles those who encounter them.

In this chapter, we will explore the characteristics of both happy and joyful individuals, how they are perceived by others, and the underlying sources of their emotions. By understanding these distinctions, we can begin to appreciate the value of striving for joy over mere happiness and embark on a journey towards a more fulfilling and resilient emotional state.

Visible Traits of Happiness vs. Joy
Typical Characteristics of a Happy Person

1. **Smiles Often:**
    - ❖ **Frequent Smiling:** A happy person often has a smile on their face, a visible indicator of their positive emotions. Alongside smiling, happy individuals usually have relaxed and open facial expressions, exuding a cheerful demeanor. Happiness often manifests as an upbeat and optimistic outlook, influencing their interactions with others. Happy individuals typically engage warmly with others, displaying a friendly and approachable nature. Smiling can be a spontaneous reaction to pleasant events or interactions, signaling to others that they are approachable and content.

❖ **Facial Expressions:** Alongside smiling, happy individuals usually have relaxed and open facial expressions. Their eyes might crinkle with delight, and their overall demeanor reflects a lighthearted attitude.

2. Appears Cheerful and Friendly:

❖ **Cheerful Demeanor:** Happiness often manifests as an upbeat and optimistic outlook. Happy people tend to radiate positivity, making them seem livelier and more enthusiastic. This cheerful disposition can be infectious, uplifting the mood of those around them.

❖ **Friendly Interactions:** Happy individuals typically engage warmly with others. They are more likely to initiate conversations, offer compliments, and show genuine interest in other people's lives. This friendliness helps them build and maintain social connections.

3. Engages in Social Activities and Celebrations:

❖ **Active Social Life:** Happiness often drives people to seek out and participate in social activities. Whether it's attending parties, joining clubs, or simply hanging out with friends, happy individuals thrive in social settings where they can share their positive energy.

❖ **Celebratory Behavior:** Happy people often participate in celebrations, whether personal milestones like birthdays and anniversaries, or communal events such as festivals and holidays They enjoy marking these occasions and often play a central role in organizing and enhancing the festive spirit.

Typical Characteristics of a Joyful Person

You may be thinking to yourself – well, Frances, I'm a bit confused. I would have thought that the traits listed for a happy person would be reflective of joy. Yes, that is true. However, below, we'll explain further the enhanced characteristics of a joyful individual, in which these traits are exhibited consistently.

1. A Twinkle in Their Eye:

- ❖ **Inner Radiance:** Joyful individuals often have a noticeable sparkle in their eyes, a sign of the inner light and deep contentment they carry within. This twinkle can be seen as a reflection of their soul, indicating an inner joy and contentment. a profound sense of peace and fulfillment.
- ❖ **Genuine Expression of Sincerity:** Unlike the sometimes-fleeting nature of a smile, the twinkle in a joyful person's eye is enduring. It persists regardless of external circumstances, revealing a deep, unshakeable joy that transcends mere momentary happiness.

2. An Extra Spring in Their Step:

- ❖ **Energetic Presence:** Joyful people move with a sense of purpose and vitality. Their steps are often buoyant, reflecting their enthusiasm for life and the inner joy that propels them forward.

- ❖ **Positive, Upbeat Body Language:** This spring in their step is accompanied by open and expressive body language. Joyful individuals tend to stand taller, move more freely, and exhibit a natural grace that draws others to them.

3. Aura of Peace and Contentment:

Calm and Composed: Joyful individuals exude a sense of calm and tranquility. Even in the midst of chaos, they remain composed, radiating inner peace that often calms those around them.

- ❖ **Enduring Positivity:** Unlike the transient nature of happiness, joy is a steady, ongoing state. Joyful people maintain a positive outlook even during challenging times, with their inner joy acting as a source of resilience and strength.

Comparison and Analysis

1. Duration and Stability:

Happiness: Typically tied to specific events or achievements, happiness can be fleeting. It is easily influenced by external factors and can diminish when circumstances change.

❖ **Joy:** Joy is stable and enduring. It is an internal state of being that persists regardless of external conditions, providing a consistent source of contentment and peace.

2. Depth and Authenticity:

❖ **Happiness:** Often surface-level, happiness can sometimes mask deeper emotions. While happy people may appear cheerful, their happiness can be situational and may not reflect their overall emotional well-being.

❖ **Joy:** Joy is profound and genuine. It stems from a deep sense of fulfillment and purpose, and is less likely to be affected by external events. Joyful people are authentically content, with their joy rooted deeply in their core being.

3. Perception by Others:

❖ **Happiness:** Generally, happy people are well-received and liked for their cheerful and friendly nature. However, their visible happiness can sometimes be seen as superficial, especially if it is overly exuberant or inconsistent.

❖ **Joy:** Joyful people often evoke mixed reactions. Some may admire and aspire to their serene and content demeanor, while others may feel envy or discomfort, particularly if they are struggling with their own emotional challenges.

Perceptions and Reactions of Others

Perceptions of Happy People

1.Generally Positive and Approachable:

- ❖ **Welcoming Presence:** Happy individuals are often seen as warm and inviting. Their frequent smiles and cheerful demeanor make them approachable and easy to talk to. This positive energy attracts others, fostering a sense of camaraderie and social connection.

- ❖ **Boosting Morale:** In both personal and professional settings, Happy individuals are often seen as warm and inviting. Their positive outlook can be contagious, creating a more pleasant and productive environment. For example, a cheerful colleague can enhance the workplace atmosphere, making it feel more enjoyable and less stressful.

2. Sometimes Seen as Superficial or Overly Positive:

Surface-Level Positivity: Although happiness is generally well-received, it can occasionally be perceived as superficial or insincere. When individuals maintain a consistently happy demeanor without acknowledging any challenges, their positivity might seem forced or artificial.

- ❖ **Ignoring Deeper Issues:** Happy individuals may sometimes be viewed as disconnected from reality if their happiness appears to gloss over genuine problems or emotional complexities. This can lead to perceptions of them avoiding deeper truths, potentially resulting in a lack of trust or respect from others.

Perceptions of Joyful People:

1. Mixed Reactions: Awe, Admiration, Envy, or Disdain:

- ❖ **Awe and Admiration:** Many people admire joyful individuals for their consistent inner peace and resilience. Joyful people often inspire others, demonstrating that it is possible to maintain a positive outlook regardless of external circumstances. Their unwavering joy can evoke admiration and respect. Their unwavering joy can evoke a sense of wonder and respect.

- ❖ **Envy and Disdain:** conversely, some may react with envy or disdain. The presence of a joyful person can highlight their own emotional struggles, leading to feelings of inadequacy or resentment. This reaction can manifest as negative comments or dismissive attitudes, such as, "What is she/he always smiling about?" This response often stems from jealousy and frustration at their own inability to achieve such a state of joy.

2. The Root of These Reactions:

- ❖ **Societal Norms:** Society often values visible and easily understandable emotions like happiness, , which align with social norms of being cheerful and agreeable. Deep joy, however, is less understood and can challenge conventional expectations. Joyful people may be perceived as unconventional because their inner peace does not fluctuate with societal pressures or trends.

❖ **Personal Insecurities:** Reactions to joyful people are frequently influenced by individual insecurities. Someone who struggles with their emotions might feel threatened or inadequate in the presence of a joyful person, leading to envy or disdain. The enduring joy of others can starkly contrast with their own struggles, provoking defensive or negative responses.

❖ **Cultural Attitudes:** Different cultures have varying attitudes towards the expression of joy and happiness. In some cultures, overt displays of joy might be celebrated and encouraged, while in others, they could be seen as inappropriate or boastful. Cultural norms can significantly influence how joyful individuals are perceived and treated.

The Source of Happiness and Joy - Examining What Typically Makes People Happy

1. External Circumstances:

- ❖ **Success:** Achieving goals, whether personal or professional, often brings a sense of happiness. Success in one's career, completing a project, or earning a promotion provides a feeling of accomplishment and pride.

Possessions: Material comforts and possessions can contribute to happiness. Owning a home, a car, or the latest gadgets can provide a sense of security and satisfaction.

- ❖ **Social Validation:** Positive feedback and recognition from others enhance happiness. Compliments, social media likes, and approval from peers or superiors boost self-esteem and contribute to a happy state.

2. Temporary Achievements and Pleasures:

- ❖ **Achievements:** Short-term successes, such as winning a game, passing an exam, or completing a challenging task, bring bursts of happiness. These achievements validate our efforts and skills, providing a temporary high.
- ❖ **Pleasures:** Enjoying life's simple pleasures like eating a favorite meal, watching a good movie, or going on a vacation also creates happiness. These experiences provide immediate gratification and sensory pleasure.

The Source of Happiness and Joy - Examining What Brings Joy to Individuals

1. Internal State of Being:

- ❖ **Inner Peace:** Joy stems from a profound sense of inner peace and contentment. This state of being is not easily swayed by external circumstances and remains constant despite life's ups and downs.
- ❖ **Emotional Resilience:** Joyful individuals possess a strong sense of emotional resilience. They can navigate challenges and setbacks with a positive outlook, maintaining their inner joy through difficult times.

2. Deep-Seeded Beliefs, Values, and a Sense of Purpose:

- ❖ **Beliefs and Values:** Joy often arises from living in alignment with one's core beliefs and values. Acting according to personal principles provides a sense of integrity and fulfillment, fostering lasting joy.
- ❖ **Sense of Purpose:** Having a clear sense of purpose and direction in life is a significant source of joy. Engaging in meaningful work, contributing to the well-being of others, or pursuing passions and hobbies that resonate deeply can create a sustained sense of joy.

3. Connection to Spirituality, Nature, or a Higher Power:

❖ **Spirituality:** For many, joy is deeply connected to their spirituality or faith. A relationship with a higher power, participation in religious practices, or meditation can foster a profound sense of joy and peace.

❖ **Nature:** Connection to nature also brings joy. Spending time outdoors, appreciating the beauty of the natural world, and experiencing the tranquility of nature can lead to a deep sense of joy and well-being.

❖ **Higher Purpose:** Feeling part of something larger than oneself, whether through community service, activism, or spiritual practices, provides a sense of belonging and fulfillment, contributing to inner joy.

Chapter Two

—— · ★ · ——

Thanks, but stay in your lane

Introduction

In Chapter 1, we expounded upon the nuanced distinction between happiness and joy, exploring how happiness is often a fleeting state, influenced by external circumstances and material comforts. On the other hand, joy is a profound, enduring state of being that emanates from within, rooted in deep-seated beliefs, values, and a sense of purpose. This understanding laid the foundation for recognizing the true essence of joy, which transcends the transient nature of happiness.

As we transition into Chapter 2, we confront a common challenge that many of us face on our journey to finding joy: dealing with unsolicited advice and opinions on personal life choices. We all know someone who feels compelled to offer their two cents on how we can improve our lives—whether it's family, friends, colleagues, or even strangers on social media. These self-appointed advisors often believe they have the key to our happiness and success, projecting their idea of perfection onto us.

However, it's essential to understand that self-appointed advisors, despite their seemingly well-meaning intentions, are not always coming from a place of complete happiness or blissful contentment themselves. In fact, they might be projecting their insecurities and unfulfilled desires onto us. This chapter will explore how to handle such unsolicited advice effectively, allowing us to stay true to our own path and maintain our focus on what genuinely brings us joy.

We'll examine the nature and motivations behind unsolicited advice, its impact on our emotional well-being and personal goals, and strategies to navigate these often un-welcome intrusions. By recognizing the underlying dynamics at play, we can learn to let others speak their minds without feeling derailed from our plans, ensuring that we continue to move towards a life of authentic joy and fulfillment.

The Nature of Unsolicited Advice

Unsolicited advice is guidance or suggestions offered without being requested. It often comes from a place of assumed authority or concern, where the advisor believes they know what is best for another person. While sometimes well-intentioned, unsolicited advice can be intrusive, unwanted, and even counterproductive.

Common Scenarios Where People Offer Unsolicited Advice

1. Social Gatherings:

❖ **Holiday Dinners:** Friends, acquaintances, family members, particularly older relatives, may feel entitled to offer advice on everything from career choices to parenting methods. These gatherings provide a forum for sharing opinions, often leading to a barrage of unsolicited guidance.

❖ **Milestones and Celebrations:** Events such as weddings, graduations, and birthdays are prime times for family members to give advice. They might suggest how to manage finances, plan for the future, or handle personal relationships, regardless of whether their input is sought.

2. Workplace or Professional Development Settings:

❖ **Colleagues and Supervisors:** In professional settings, coworkers, leaders, and manager may offer unsolicited advice on work habits, career progression, or personal development. This can stem from a genuine desire to help or from a place of competition and self-interest and is often appropriate

❖ **Performance Reviews:** While some feedback is necessary and constructive, performance reviews can sometimes include unsolicited advice that goes beyond

- 20 -

professional development, encroaching on personal areas such as work-life balance or personal style.

3. Social Media:

- ❖ **Public Platforms:** Social media is a hotbed for unsolicited advice, expression of one's thoughts and opinions. When individuals share aspects of their lives online, they often receive comments and messages offering suggestions on everything from health and fitness to parenting and lifestyle choices.

- ❖ **Online Communities:** Participating in forums, groups, or online communities can expose individuals to a plethora of unsolicited advice. While these spaces are meant for support and sharing, they can quickly become overwhelming with opinions and recommendations from strangers.

Unsolicited advice can be particularly challenging because it often comes at a time when individuals are not seeking guidance or may already feel vulnerable. Understanding the nature and common scenarios of unsolicited advice is the first step in learning how to handle it effectively, ensuring that we stay true to our own paths and maintain our focus on personal joy and fulfillment.

The Motivations Behind Giving Unsolicited Advice

Understanding why people feel compelled to offer unsolicited advice can help us better manage and respond to it. Here are some key motivations:

Desire to Help and Feel Useful:

Many individuals give unsolicited advice out of a genuine desire to help. They believe that their experience or knowledge can benefit others, and they want to contribute positively to someone's life. This motivation is often rooted in empathy and compassion. For example, a parent might offer advice to their adult child about managing finances or relationships, sincerely hoping to make their child's life easier and more successful. Similarly, a colleague might suggest a more efficient way to complete a task, aiming to assist rather than criticize.

Additionally, giving advice can make the advisor feel useful and valued. It can provide a sense of purpose, especially if they see the recipient acting on their suggestions and achieving positive outcomes. This feeling of contributing to someone else's well-being can be a powerful motivator.

Projection of Personal Insecurities and Unfulfilled Desires:

Unsolicited advice can also stem from the advisor's own insecurities and unfulfilled desires. People often project their fears, regrets, and unachieved goals onto others. For instance, someone who struggled with their career might give persistent advice about job choices, projecting their own anxieties and desires for success onto the recipient.

This projection allows the advisor to address their own unresolved issues indirectly. By advising others, they feel as though they are correcting their past mistakes or achieving vicariously through someone else. Unfortunately, this type of advice is often less about the recipient's needs and more about the advisor's need to cope with their own insecurities.

Social Norms and Cultural Influences:

Cultural norms and societal expectations can also play a significant role in the prevalence of unsolicited advice. In some cultures, giving advice is seen as a sign of care and involvement.

Elders, in particular, may feel it is their duty to impart wisdom and guidance to younger generations. This cultural expectation can make unsolicited advice a routine part of social interactions, especially within families and close-knit communities.

In broader society, the rise of social media and digital communication has amplified the tendency to offer advice. Online platforms encourage sharing opinions and experiences, often blurring the lines between solicited and unsolicited advice. The ease of commenting on someone's post or sending a direct message can make giving advice almost reflexive, even when it is not requested.

Moreover, the societal pressure to appear knowledgeable and competent can drive people to offer advice as a way to assert their expertise and gain social validation. This behavior is often reinforced by the belief that sharing advice, even unsolicited, is a demonstration of intelligence and insight.

The Impact of Unsolicited Advice on Individuals

Unsolicited advice can have a range of impacts on individuals, affecting their emotions, goals, relationships, and self-esteem. Understanding these impacts can help us develop strategies to cope with and respond to such advice effectively.

Emotional Responses to Unsolicited Advice:

1. Frustration:

- ❖ **Feeling Undermined:** Receiving unsolicited advice can be frustrating, especially when it feels like the advisor is questioning your judgment or capabilities. This sense of being undermined can lead to irritation and annoyance.

- ❖ **Interruption of Flow:** When you are focused on your goals and someone interjects with unrequested advice, it can disrupt your momentum and create unnecessary obstacles, adding to the frustration.

2. Self-Doubt:

- ❖ **Questioning Decisions:** Unsolicited advice can cause you to second-guess your choices and abilities. Even if you were confident in your path, persistent advice can plant seeds of doubt, making you wonder if you are on the right track.
- ❖ **Eroding Confidence:** Over time, repeated unsolicited advice can erode your self-confidence. When others frequently suggest different ways of doing things, it can make you feel less capable and less sure of your decisions.

3. Resentment:

- ❖ **Feeling Overwhelmed:** Constant advice, particularly when unsolicited, can lead to feelings of resentment towards the advisor. This is especially true if the advice feels more critical than constructive.
- ❖ **Loss of Autonomy:** Unsolicited advice can make you feel like you are not in control of your own life. This loss of autonomy can breed resentment, as it feels like others are trying to dictate your actions and choices.

How Unsolicited Advice Can Derail Personal Goals and Plans

1. Distraction and Confusion:

- ❖ **Shift in Focus:** Unsolicited advice can distract you from your original goals. When you start considering others' opinions, you may lose sight of your own objectives, leading to a shift in focus that can derail your plans.

- ❖ **Conflicting Opinions:** Receiving advice from multiple sources can create confusion, especially if the advice is contradictory. This conflicting input can make it difficult to make decisions and stay on course.

2. Delayed Progress:

- ❖ **Indecisiveness:** The self-doubt and confusion caused by unsolicited advice can lead to indecision. When you are unsure of what path to take, you may hesitate or procrastinate, delaying progress towards your goals.

- ❖ **Unnecessary Changes:** In an attempt to accommodate others' advice, you might make unnecessary changes to your plans. These adjustments can divert your efforts and resources, slowing down your overall progress.

The Effect on Relationships and Self-Esteem

1. Strained Relationships:

- ❖ **Tension and Conflict:** Constant unsolicited advice can create tension and conflict in relationships. Whether it's with family, friends, or colleagues, persistent advice can lead to arguments and strained interactions.
- ❖ **Diminished Trust:** When someone frequently gives unsolicited advice, it can diminish trust in the relationship. You might feel that the advisor does not respect your autonomy or trust your judgment, leading to a breakdown in mutual respect.

2. Impact on Self-Esteem:

- ❖ **Feeling Inadequate:** Unsolicited advice can make you feel inadequate or not good enough. When others suggest different ways of doing things, it can imply that your current efforts are insufficient, impacting your self-esteem.
- ❖ **Reduced Self-Worth:** Over time, the accumulation of unsolicited advice can reduce your sense of self-worth. When you internalize the notion that others know better than you, it can weaken your confidence and belief in your abilities.

Identifying the Source: Who Are These Advisors?

Unsolicited advice can come from various sources, each with different motivations and characteristics. Recognizing who these advisors are and understanding their intentions can help us navigate their advice more effectively.

Characteristics of People Who Frequently Give Unsolicited Advice

1. Close Family Members and Friends:

- ❖ **Parents and Relatives:** Family members, especially parents, often feel a sense of responsibility to guide and protect their loved ones. This can lead to frequent unsolicited advice on everything from career choices to personal relationships.

- ❖ **Close Friends:** Friends who care deeply about us might offer unsolicited advice out of concern. They may believe they have valuable insights to share based on their experiences and observations.

2. Colleagues and Acquaintances:

- ❖ **Workplace Advisors:** In a professional setting, colleagues and supervisors might offer unsolicited advice related to job performance, career development, or work-life balance. This advice can stem from a desire to help or from a need to assert authority.

- ❖ **Casual Acquaintances:** People we interact with occasionally, such as neighbors or casual friends, might give unsolicited advice based on limited knowledge of our lives.

Their suggestions often come from a place of assumed understanding rather than genuine insight.

3. Strangers and Online Commenters:

- ❖ **Social Media Users:** The anonymity and reach of social media platforms enable strangers to offer unsolicited advice freely. When individuals share aspects of their lives online, they open themselves up to comments and suggestions from people they do not know.

- ❖ **Public Figures and Influencers:** Sometimes, public figures or influencers might offer unsolicited advice to their followers. While their intentions might be to inspire or help, their advice can feel impersonal and generic.

Understanding Their Intentions: Well-Meaning vs. Critical and Controlling

1. Well-Meaning Intentions:

- ❖ **Genuine Concern:** Many people offer unsolicited advice because they genuinely care about the recipient's well-being. They believe their guidance can help avoid mistakes and lead to better outcomes.

- ❖ **Sharing Experiences:** Well-meaning advisors often share advice based on their personal experiences. They want to pass on lessons they've learned, hoping to spare others from similar challenges.

❖ **Desire to Support:** Some advisors aim to provide support and encouragement. Their advice is meant to empower and uplift, even if it comes across as unsolicited.

2. Critical and Controlling Intentions:

❖ **Asserting Authority:** Individuals who feel the need to assert their authority might give unsolicited advice to demonstrate their knowledge or superiority. This can be common in hierarchical relationships, such as between supervisors and employees.

❖ **Projection of Insecurities:** Advisors with critical or controlling intentions might project their insecurities onto others. They offer advice as a way to manage their own anxieties and fears, often without considering the recipient's perspective.

Need for Control: Some individuals give unsolicited advice to exert control over others. They may have a controlling personality and believe they know what is best for everyone. This can lead to advice that feels more like commands than suggestions.

The Advisor's Own Happiness and Joy

Understanding the advisor's state of contentment and fulfillment can shed light on their motivations for giving unsolicited advice. Often, their own struggles and dissatisfaction play a significant role in driving their behavior, highlighting the irony of taking advice from someone who is not fully happy with their own life.

Analyzing the Advisor's State of Contentment and Fulfillment

1. Surface-Level Happiness

- ❖ **Outward Appearance vs. Inner Peace:** Advisors often appear content on the surface, presenting a façade of stability and success. However, their true state of mind may be far more complex and conflicted. They may maintain an image of happiness, masking underlying insecurities or unfulfilled desires.

- ❖ **Desire for Validation:** Individuals who frequently offer unsolicited advice might seek validation for their own choices and beliefs. By advising others, they attempt to reaffirm their life decisions, projecting a sense of contentment that they may not genuinely feel.

2. Internal Struggles and Dissatisfaction:

- ❖ **Unresolved Issues:** Many advisors grapple with unresolved personal issues. Their need to offer advice can stem from a subconscious desire to address their own regrets and mistakes through others. For instance, someone who faced career failures might advise others obsessively about job choices, attempting to rewrite their own history.

❖ **Unmet Aspirations:** Advisors might have unfulfilled aspirations or goals they never achieved. This sense of dissatisfaction can drive them to push others towards paths they wish they had taken. Their advice often reflects their own unachieved dreams and the longing for a different outcome.

How Their Own Struggles and Dissatisfaction May Drive Their Behavior

1. Projection of Insecurities:

❖ **Externalizing Internal Conflicts:** Advisors often project their insecurities onto others, offering advice as a means to cope with their own fears and anxieties. This projection allows them to externalize their internal conflicts, giving them a sense of control over situations that they feel powerless about in their own lives.

❖ **Seeking Redemption:** By advising others, individuals attempt to seek redemption for their perceived failures. They believe that if they can help someone avoid the same pitfalls, it will somehow rectify their own past mistakes.

2. Need for Control:

- ❖ **Compensating for Lack of Control:** Advisors who struggle with their own lives might seek to exert control over others as a compensatory mechanism. By dictating what others should do, they momentarily alleviate their own sense of powerlessness and dissatisfaction.

- ❖ **Influence and Authority:** Giving advice can provide a sense of influence and authority. For individuals who feel marginalized or undervalued, advising others can be a way to assert their importance and relevance.

The Irony of Taking Advice from Someone Who Is Not Fully Happy with Their Own Life

1. Questioning Credibility:

- ❖ **Lack of Authentic Experience:** Taking advice from someone who is not fully happy with their own life is inherently ironic. Their guidance lacks the authenticity and insight that come from genuine contentment and fulfillment. It raises questions about the credibility of their advice and its applicability to your own situation.

- ❖ **Misaligned Values:** Advisors who are not at peace with their own lives may have values and priorities that differ significantly from yours. Their advice might reflect their own coping mechanisms rather than universal truths, leading to misaligned guidance that does not resonate with your personal goals.

2. Learning from Their Mistakes:

- ❖ **Observing Outcomes:** Instead of taking advice from those who are not fully happy, it can be more beneficial to observe their outcomes and learn from their mistakes. Understanding the consequences of their choices can provide valuable insights without directly following their guidance.
- ❖ **Empathy and Understanding:** Recognizing the struggles of advisors can foster empathy and understanding. By seeing their advice as a reflection of their own challenges, you can better appreciate their perspective without feeling compelled to act on their suggestions.

Strategies for Dealing with Unsolicited Advice

Unsolicited advice can be challenging to manage, but there are effective strategies to handle it while maintaining your own peace and focus. These strategies include developing a thick skin, using polite responses and assertive communication techniques, and setting boundaries to stay true to your personal goals.

Developing a Thick Skin: Learning to Ignore or Deflect Unwanted Opinion

1.Emotional Resilience:

- ❖ **Understanding Intentions:** Recognize that unsolicited advice often comes from a place of concern or the advisor's need to feel useful. Understanding this can help you take their comments less personally and reduce the emotional impact.
- ❖ **Self-Confidence:** Strengthening your self-confidence can help you remain unaffected by unsolicited advice. Believing in your decisions and capabilities allows you to brush off opinions that do not align with your values and goals.

2. Selective Listening:

- ❖ **Filtering Advice:** Not all unsolicited advice needs to be taken seriously. Develop the habit of filtering out advice that is irrelevant or unhelpful while considering only those suggestions that might genuinely benefit you.
- ❖ **Mental Deflection:** Practice mentally deflecting unwanted advice by focusing on your own thoughts and plans. Remind yourself of your goals and the reasons behind your choices to stay grounded.

Polite Responses and Assertive Communication Techniques

1. Polite Deflections:

- ❖ **Thanking and Redirecting:** Acknowledge the advice politely and then steer the conversation in another direction. For example, "Thank you for your suggestion. I'll think about it. By the way, have you heard about...?"
- ❖ **Neutral Responses:** Use neutral responses to acknowledge advice without committing to it. Phrases like "I'll consider that" or "That's an interesting point" can be useful.

2. Assertive Communication:

- ❖ **Expressing Boundaries:** Clearly and respectfully communicate your boundaries. For instance, "I appreciate your concern, but I prefer to handle this my way."
- ❖ **Stating Preferences:** Assertively express your preferences and decisions. Use "I" statements to take ownership of your choices, such as "I've decided to approach this differently based on what works best for me."

Setting Boundaries and Maintaining Focus on Personal Goals

1. Establishing Clear Boundaries:

- ❖ **Identifying Limits:** Determine what types of advice you are open to and what you consider off-limits. Communicate these limits to those around you when necessary.

❖ **Consistent Reinforcement:** Consistently reinforce your boundaries by gently reminding people when they overstep. For example, "I appreciate your input, but I'd like to stick to my own plan."

2. Maintaining Focus on Personal Goals:

❖ **Prioritizing Goals:** Keep your personal goals at the forefront of your mind. Regularly remind yourself of your objectives and the reasons behind your decisions to stay focused.

❖ **Creating a Supportive Environment:** Surround yourself with supportive individuals who respect your choices and encourage your autonomy. Minimize interactions with those who frequently offer unsolicited advice.

3. Self-Reflection and Adjustment:

❖ **Regular Self-Assessment:** Periodically assess your progress towards your goals and reflect on the advice you've received. This can help you determine if any unsolicited advice might actually be useful without feeling pressured to act on it immediately.

❖ **Adaptive Strategies:** Be flexible and willing to adapt your strategies if necessary, but ensure that any changes align with your core values and long-term objectives.

The Importance of Following Your Own Path

In a world filled with varied opinions and advice, staying true to your own path is crucial for personal fulfillment, joy and success. Trusting your instincts and inner wisdom, valuing personal growth and self-discovery, and learning from stories of individuals who succeeded by being authentic can provide the inspiration and confidence needed to navigate life's journey.

Trusting Your Instincts and Inner Wisdom

1. Innate Guidance:

- ❖ **Intuitive Insight:** Each person has an inner compass that guides them towards their true desires and goals. Trusting your instincts allows you to tap into this intuitive insight, leading to decisions that are aligned with your authentic self.

- ❖ **Personal Experience:** Your instincts are shaped by your unique experiences and knowledge. Relying on them helps you draw from a well of personal wisdom that external advice may not fully understand or appreciate.

2. Building Confidence:

- ❖ **Self-Reliance:** Trusting your instincts fosters self-reliance and confidence in your decision-making abilities. It empowers you to take ownership of your life and make choices that reflect your true aspirations.

- ❖ **Overcoming Doubt:** By consistently trusting and acting on your inner wisdom, you gradually overcome self-doubt and build a stronger sense of self-assurance. This resilience is essential for navigating challenges and setbacks.

The Value of Personal Growth and Self-Discovery

1. Learning and Evolving:

- ❖ **Continuous Improvement:** Following your own path encourages ongoing personal growth. Each decision and experience contribute to your evolution, helping you become a more knowledgeable and capable individual.
- ❖ **Embracing Challenges:** Personal growth often involves facing and overcoming challenges. These experiences teach resilience, adaptability, and problem-solving skills that are crucial for long-term success.

2. Authenticity and Fulfillment:

- ❖ **True Happiness:** Authenticity leads to genuine happiness and fulfillment. When you live in accordance with your true self, you experience a deeper sense of satisfaction and joy that external validation cannot provide.
- ❖ **Unique Contribution:** By staying true to yourself, you bring a unique perspective and set of talents to the world. This authenticity allows you to make a meaningful and distinctive contribution to your community and society.

Chapter Three

—— ⋆ ——

Where there's a will, there's a way

Introduction

Will-power and determination - The journey towards achieving our dreams and overcoming obstacles is seldom straightforward. It demands an unwavering commitment to our goals and the resilience to push through adversity. This chapter explores how a strong will and resolute determination can serve as the driving force behind remarkable achievements and personal growth.

Whether you're pursuing a career change, setting ambitious goals, or striving to overcome personal hurdles, remember: with determination, anything is possible. By embracing the principles of willpower and determination, we can pave the way for success and fulfillment, no matter how daunting the path may seem.

The Power of Visualizing Goals, Dreams, and Ambitions

Visualization is a powerful tool that can significantly enhance your ability to achieve your goals. By creating a mental image of what you want to accomplish, you set a clear and tangible target for your efforts. Visualization helps bridge the gap between where you are and where you want to be, making your dreams and ambitions feel more attainable. It reinforces your commitment and provides a constant reminder of what you are striving for.

Practice of Posting Goals

One effective way to harness the power of visualization is by posting your goals where you can see them every day. This could be on a mirror, a door, in a journal, or any other prominent place in your home. By doing so, you create a physical representation of your aspirations that serves as a daily reminder of what you are working towards. This practice keeps your goals at the forefront of your mind, motivating you to take consistent action.

In my own experience, I have found that keeping my goals visible has been instrumental in my success. I have my goals posted on my office, written in my journals, and taped on my closet door, where I see them every morning as I start my day and every evening as I wind down. I also create notes in my phone, tying scriptures and the promises of

God as reminders I can meditate on daily. This simple practice has made a significant difference in my ability to stay focused and motivated. Each time I see those goals, I am reminded of my purpose and the steps I need to take to achieve them. Not only that, but as I meet quarterly, semiannual, and/or annual goals, I check them off and celebrate - the small and large achievements.

Benefits of Daily Visual Reminders

1. Constant Motivation: Daily visual reminders keep your goals top of mind, providing a continuous source of motivation. They serve as a daily nudge, encouraging you to stay on track and make progress, no matter how small.

2. Reinforced Focus and Priority: When your goals are constantly visible, they naturally become a priority. You are more likely to make decisions and take actions that align with your aspirations. This focus helps you allocate your time and resources more effectively towards achieving your objectives.

3. Increased Accountability: Seeing your goals every day creates a sense of accountability. It is a reminder of the commitment you have made to yourself. This accountability can be a powerful motivator, especially during times when you might feel discouraged or distracted.

The Psychological Impact of Visualization on Motivation and Determination

Visualization has a profound psychological impact that can significantly boost your motivation and determination. Here's how:

1. Enhanced Clarity: Visualization helps clarify what you want to achieve. By creating a clear mental image of your goals, you gain a better understanding of what success looks like. This clarity makes it easier to identify the steps you need to take and the resources you need to gather.

2. Positive Reinforcement: Each time you visualize your goals, you reinforce a positive belief in your ability to achieve them. This positive reinforcement builds your confidence and reduces self-doubt, making it easier to take action and persist through challenges.

3. Emotional Connection: Visualizing your goals creates an emotional connection to them. You begin to feel the excitement and satisfaction that comes with achieving your aspirations. This emotional connection strengthens your desire to reach your goals, fueling your determination to overcome obstacles.

4. Mental Rehearsal: Visualization acts as a form of mental rehearsal. By repeatedly picturing yourself achieving your goals, you train your mind to perform the necessary actions. This mental practice can enhance your skills, improve your performance, and increase your chances of success.

Setting Deadlines and How to Handle Missed Targets

Encourage Setting Dates for Goal Completion

Setting deadlines for your goals is an essential step in turning your aspirations into reality. Deadlines provide structure and a sense of urgency, helping to break down your larger objectives into manageable tasks. By assigning specific dates to your goals, you create a timeline that guides your actions and keeps you accountable. This approach transforms vague ambitions into concrete plans, making it easier to track progress and stay focused.

Address the Common Fear of Not Meeting Deadlines

A common fear that many people face is the anxiety of not meeting their deadlines. This fear can be paralyzing, leading to procrastination and self-doubt. It's important to recognize that this fear is a natural part of the goal-setting process. Understanding that deadlines are tools for motivation, not measures of failure, can help alleviate this anxiety.

Be realistic with timelines needed to accomplish goals successfully. The key is to view deadlines as flexible milestones rather than rigid endpoints. If necessary, tell a trusted friend, acquaintance, or colleague about your goal and timeline for additional motivation and quite frankly, enhanced healthy pressure. Have them check-in with you, and if 'life' happens, causing natural delays, have grace with yourself and get back on track!

Offer Reassurance: Missing a Deadline Is Not a Failure but an Opportunity to Adjust

Missing a deadline is not an indication of failure; rather, it is an opportunity to reassess and adjust your approach. Life is unpredictable, and circumstances can change, making it challenging to adhere to initial timelines.

When you miss a deadline, take a step back and evaluate what factors contributed to the delay. This reflection allows you to learn from the experience, refine your strategy, and set a new, more realistic deadline. Remember, the goal remains the same, but the path to achieving it may need adjustment.

Strategies for Maintaining Motivation After Missing a Deadline

1. Reflect and Learn: Analyze why you missed the deadline. Identify any obstacles or inefficiencies in your process. Use this insight to improve your approach and avoid similar issues in the future.

2. Adjust Your Plan: Revise your timeline and break down your goals into smaller, more manageable tasks. This can make the overall objective feel less daunting and help you regain momentum.

3. Celebrate Progress: Acknowledge the progress you have made, even if you haven't reached the final goal. Celebrating small wins can boost your motivation and remind you of how far you've come.

4. Stay Positive: Maintain a positive mindset. Focus on the journey and the growth you experience along the way, rather than fixating on the missed deadline.

Keep the Goal Posted and Move It to a New Timeframe

When you miss a deadline, it's crucial to keep the goal visible and relevant. Rather than discarding the goal, simply move it to a new timeframe.

This practice reinforces your commitment and keeps the goal in your line of sight. By adjusting the deadline, you reaffirm your dedication to achieving the goal, demonstrating resilience and adaptability.

Emphasize Persistence and the Likelihood of Eventual Success

Persistence is the cornerstone of achieving any goal. The journey to success is rarely a straight path; it is filled with twists, turns, and setbacks. By staying persistent, you increase the likelihood of eventual success. Each step forward, no matter how small, brings you closer to your objective.

1. Stay Committed: Maintain your dedication to the goal, regardless of setbacks. Commitment fuels perseverance, helping you push through challenges.

2. Adapt and Overcome: Be willing to adapt your approach as needed. Flexibility in your strategy allows you to overcome obstacles and continue progressing.

3. Focus on the Long-Term Vision: Keep the bigger picture in mind. Remember why you set the goal in the first place and let that vision drive your persistence.

Career Exploration and Reinvention

Encourage Readers to Discover Their True Career Passions

Finding a career that truly aligns with your passions can be a transformative experience. It's essential to explore what genuinely excites and motivates you, beyond just financial considerations.

Take time to reflect on your interests, skills, and values. Ask yourself what activities make you lose track of time or what you would do even if you weren't paid for it. Understanding your passions is the first step towards a fulfilling career.

Advice on Leaving Dead-End Jobs

Staying in a dead-end job can drain your energy and stifle your potential. If you find yourself in a position that offers no room for growth, creativity, or satisfaction, it might be time to consider moving on. Leaving a secure but unfulfilling job can be daunting, but it is crucial for your long-term happiness and career satisfaction. Start by planning your exit strategy: save money, update your resume, talk to a career coach, and network within your desired field. Your current job doesn't define your future; take control and seek opportunities that align with your aspirations.

Strategies for Exploring New Career Paths

1. Research and Self-Assessment: Conduct thorough research on potential career paths. Use tools like career assessments and personality tests to understand where your strengths and interests lie.

2. Informational Interviews: Reach out to professionals in fields you're interested in. Conduct informational interviews to gain insights into their daily responsibilities, challenges, and required skills.

3. Volunteer or Intern: If possible, volunteer or intern in your field of interest. This hands-on experience can provide valuable insights and help you determine if it's the right fit for you.

4. Online Courses and Workshops: Enroll in online courses, workshops, or certificate programs to gain new skills and knowledge. Many platforms offer affordable or free courses on a wide range of subjects.

Addressing Boredom and Dissatisfaction in Established Careers

Even in established careers, it's common to feel bored or dissatisfied at times. Here's how to address these feelings:

1. Seek New Challenges: Look for opportunities within your current role to take on new projects or responsibilities. This can reignite your interest and provide a sense of purpose.

2. Continued Education: Pursue further education or training to enhance your skills and open up new career opportunities within your field.

3. Mentorship and Networking: Connect with mentors or join professional networks to gain new perspectives and advice on advancing your career.

4. Career Sabbatical: Consider taking a career sabbatical if feasible. A break can provide clarity and a fresh outlook on your career.

Steps to Take for Career Change and Re-Education

1. Identify Your Goals: Clearly define what you want to achieve with your career change. Set specific, measurable, attainable, relevant, and time-bound (SMART) goals.

2. Research: Gather information about your new career path. Understand the necessary qualifications, job market trends, and potential employers.

3. Skill Development: Identify any skills gaps and seek relevant training or education. This might include returning to school, taking online courses, or gaining certifications.

4. Network: Build a network in your desired industry. Attend industry events, join professional organizations, and connect with people on LinkedIn.

5. Practical Experience: Gain practical experience through internships, part-time work, or volunteer positions. This not only enhances your resume but also helps you decide if the new career is right for you.

6. Update Your Resume and LinkedIn: Tailor your resume and LinkedIn profile to highlight relevant skills and experiences for your new career path.

7. Apply and Interview: Start applying for jobs in your new field. Prepare thoroughly for interviews by practicing responses to common questions and showcasing how your skills are transferable.

The Importance of Not Making Excuses and Taking Proactive Steps:

Excuses are the barriers that stand between you and your dreams. It's easy to get caught up in reasons why you can't pursue a career change - lack of time, fear of failure, financial constraints, or age. However, these are often rooted in fear and self-doubt. To move forward:

1. Adopt a Growth Mindset: Believe that your abilities and intelligence can be developed through dedication and hard work.

2. Take Small Steps: Break down your career change into smaller, manageable steps. This makes the process less overwhelming and keeps you moving forward.

3. Stay Committed: Remain dedicated to your goals, even when progress seems slow or challenging. Persistence is key to overcoming obstacles.

4. Seek Support: Surround yourself with supportive people who encourage and believe in you. This could be friends, family, or professional mentors.

Reiterate the Central Message: Where There's a Will, There's a Way

Regardless of age or circumstances, the adage "where there's a will, there's a way" holds true. Your determination and willingness to pursue your dreams are the most critical factors in achieving success. Embrace the journey of career exploration and reinvention with confidence and resilience. Remember, countless individuals have successfully navigated career changes, and you can too. With a clear vision, strategic planning, and unwavering determination, you can create a career that brings you joy and fulfillment.

Chapter Four

———— ⋆ ————

Zephaniah 3:17

Introduction

One of my favorite scriptures is Zephaniah 3:17!

The New Living Translation of the Bible states - "The Lord your God is with you, the Mighty Warrior who saves. He will take great delight in you; in his love, rejoice and sings praises over you with gladness."

Zephaniah 3:17 paints a vivid picture of a God who is not only mighty and capable of saving but also deeply affectionate and personally invested in His creation. The image of God rejoicing over us with singing is both humbling and uplifting. It suggests a level of intimacy and care that transcends mere obligation, revealing a God who delights in us, celebrates us, and continuously pours out His love in ways that are both profound and personal. How can that not make you smile? It simply brings peace and joy to my spirit.

Understanding that God, sings praises over us night and day is a transformative realization. It challenges us to reconsider how we view ourselves, our worth, and our relationship with the divine.

If we truly grasp the reality of God's delight in us, it raises an important question: why do we fret? Why do we allow worry and anxiety to overshadow the truth of God's unwavering love and praise? This chapter invites you to ponder these questions, to meditate on the depth of God's love, and to embrace the assurance that comes from knowing He is always rejoicing over you, providing for you, and cheering you on!

Understanding Zephaniah 3:17

Zephaniah 3:17

Explanation of the Verse and Its Promises

Zephaniah 3:17 is a verse rich with reassurance and profound significance for believers. It speaks to several core truths about God's nature and His relationship with us:

1. God's Loving Presence: "The Lord your God is with you." This phrase emphasizes God's constant presence in our lives. He is not a distant deity but one who is intimately involved in our daily existence. His presence offers comfort, guidance, and assurance that we are never alone.

2. God's Delight in Us: "He will take great delight in you." This part of the verse underscores the depth of God's affection for us. It's not just a passive love but an active delight, suggesting that God finds joy and pleasure in our existence and in our relationship with Him.

3. God's Joyful Expression: "He will rejoice over you with singing." This beautiful image conveys the extent of God's joy in us. The idea of God singing over us is a powerful testament to how deeply He values and cherishes us. It's a celebration of our relationship with Him, a divine affirmation of our worth and significance.

Significance of the Names of God

If you are a believer, understanding the Names of God provide clarity, peace, and joy over life's circumstances. Here are a few that I meditate on constantly:

1. Jehovah Nissi - the Lord your Banner, He sings praises over you daily, covers you and protects - mind, body, and spirit.

2. Jehovah Jireh - God is a provider and will do so in any area that you desire - resources, wisdom, a sound mind, et al.

3. Jehovah Shalom - He offers peace that surpasses all understanding

4. Jehovah Rapha - He is a healer and can restore every cell and neuron to great vitality.

5. El Roi - He sees you and knows your every need.

6. Adonai - The Lord of Lords - He orders your steps and provides divine direction.

7. El Shaddai (The Almighty God): reflective of God's ultimate power, sovereignty, and sufficiency. It underscores that God's might and love are limitless, providing us with everything we need.

For Believers:

Understanding Zephaniah 3:17 and the names of God mentioned within it has profound implications on how we see and experience life. It calls us to live with a heightened awareness of God's continuous presence and active involvement in our lives.

It challenges us to trust in His protection and to embrace His love and delight in us, despite our imperfections. This understanding also encourages us to find our identity and worth in the fact that God rejoices over us, which can transform how we view ourselves and our circumstances.

By meditating on Zephaniah 3:17, we are reminded that we are deeply loved, constantly protected, and joyously celebrated by the Almighty God.

This realization can help us combat fear, anxiety, and feelings of inadequacy, empowering us to live with confidence and purpose.

God Sings Praises Over <u>You!</u>

The notion that God sings praises over His people is a deeply comforting and profound truth found in Zephaniah 3:17. The imagery of God singing over us signifies His delight, joy, and celebration in His relationship with each individual believer. It goes beyond mere acknowledgment or affection; it expresses a heartfelt expression of love and affirmation from the Creator to His creation.

In many cultures and traditions, singing is often associated with joy, celebration, and expressing deep emotions. When applied to God, who is described as the Almighty and the source of all goodness, this image reveals His intimate connection with us. It portrays God not only as a distant deity but as a loving Father who takes personal pleasure in His children.

God's praise and love are not sporadic or conditional but continuous and unwavering. The phrase "night and day" in Zephaniah 3:17 emphasizes the constancy of God's affection and affirmation. It signifies that God's love for us is not limited by time or circumstance but is eternal and enduring. Whether we are aware of it or not, God is continuously rejoicing over us, singing songs of love, hope, and encouragement into our lives.

This continuous nature of God's praise and love underscores His faithfulness and commitment to His people. It serves as a reminder that His affection for us is not dependent on our performance or merit but is rooted in His character of love and grace.

The idea that God sings praises over us has profound personal implications. It challenges us to view ourselves through the lens of God's unconditional love and acceptance. It invites us to embrace our identity as beloved children of God, worthy of His joy and celebration. This realization can bring deep comfort, confidence, and assurance in our relationship with Him.

Understanding that God, the Almighty, is personally invested in each individual highlights the uniqueness and significance of our lives. It affirms that we are not insignificant or overlooked but are cherished and valued by the Creator of the universe. This awareness can transform our perspective on life's challenges, giving us strength and resilience to face difficulties with the knowledge that God is with us, rejoicing over us with singing.

Reflecting and Meditating on God's Praises

Reflecting on the truth that God sings praises over us is a powerful invitation to engage deeply with His love and affirmation. It prompts us to move beyond a surface understanding to a profound awareness of God's personal investment in our lives. Here are some ways to encourage deeper reflection:

1. Prayer: Set aside intentional time to sit quietly in God's presence. Invite Him to reveal His love and affirmation to you. Allow space for His truth to sink deeply into your heart.

2. Scripture Meditation: Meditate on verses that emphasize God's love and care for His people, such as Zephaniah 3:17. Read these passages slowly, pondering each word and allowing them to resonate with your spirit.

3. Personal Reflection: Journal your thoughts and emotions as you consider the concept of God singing praises over you. Write down instances where you have felt God's presence and affirmation in your life.

Practical Ways to Meditate

1. Daily Reflection: Start or end your day with a moment of reflection on God's love. Consider how His continuous praise over you shapes your identity and perspective.

2. Prayer of Gratitude: Develop a habit of thanking God for His love and affirmation. Express gratitude for specific moments where you had sensed His presence and encouragement.

3. Journaling: Keep a gratitude journal where you write down instances of God's faithfulness and love in your life. Reflect on how His praise strengthens your faith and confidence.

Transformative Power of Internalizing God's Love and Praise

Internalizing the truth that God sings praises over us has transformative effects on our spiritual, emotional, and mental well-being:

- ❖ **Identity and Worth:** God's words reinforce our worth and significance in His eyes, counteracting any feelings of insecurity, fear, or inadequacy.

- ❖ **Peace and Assurance:** Internalizing God's love and praise brings a deep sense of peace and assurance. It reminds us that we are not alone in our journey but are constantly supported and cherished by the Almighty.

- ❖ **Strength and Resilience:** Knowing that God rejoices over us with singing gives us strength to face challenges and adversity. It instills resilience and courage to navigate life's uncertainties with confidence in His love.

- ❖ **Spiritual Growth:** Meditating on God's praises fosters spiritual growth and maturity. It deepens our intimacy with God as we cultivate a deeper awareness of His presence and affirmation in our lives.

The Bible as Truth

Affirming the Ultimate Source of Truth

The Bible stands as the ultimate source of truth for believers, serving as God's inspired word and revelation to humanity. It encompasses timeless truths, moral teachings, historical accounts, prophecies, and guidance for living a righteous life. Throughout history, its reliability and authenticity have been affirmed by scholars, theologians, and believers alike.

Trusting in Promises and Declarations

Believers can trust in the promises and declarations found in Scripture due to its divine origin and authority. The Bible declares itself as God-breathed (2 Timothy 3:16), meaning it is inspired by God and carries His authority. Therefore, every promise, prophecy, and teaching within its pages is trustworthy and reliable.

Scripture's consistency and coherence across diverse authors, cultures, and time periods attest to its divine authorship. From the prophecies fulfilled in Jesus Christ to the ethical teachings that transcend cultural boundaries, the Bible's unified message points to its supernatural origin and enduring relevance.

Comfort and Assurance

Understanding the Bible as truth provides profound comfort and assurance to believers in several ways:

1. Steadfast Promises: The Bible contains promises of God's faithfulness, provision, and protection for His people (e.g., Psalm 23:4; Isaiah 41:10). Believers find comfort knowing that God's promises are unchanging and reliable in every circumstance.

2. Divine Guidance: Scripture offers wisdom and guidance for navigating life's challenges and decisions (e.g., Proverbs 3:5-6). By aligning their lives with biblical principles, believers find assurance in making sound choices that honor God.

3. Spiritual Reassurance: Through the narratives of faith, perseverance, and redemption found in the Bible (e.g., Hebrews 11), believers are reassured of God's sovereignty and grace. These stories inspire hope and strengthen faith during trials.

4. Eternal Perspective: The Bible provides a framework for understanding life's purpose and the promise of eternal life through Jesus Christ (e.g., John 3:16). Believers find assurance in the hope of salvation and the assurance of God's ultimate victory over sin and death.

Addressing Worry and Anxiety

Connecting God's Praise to Worry and Anxiety

The truth that God sings praises over His people provides a powerful antidote to worry and anxiety. Despite knowing intellectually that God loves and cares for us, many still struggle with anxiety. This disconnect often stems from focusing more on circumstances than on God's unwavering love and promises. However, understanding that God delights in us and rejoices over us with singing can shift our perspective. It reminds us that we are deeply valued and secure in His care, regardless of life's uncertainties.

Common Reasons for Fretting Despite God's Love

People may fret despite knowing God's love for several reasons:

1. Focus on Circumstances: When faced with challenges or uncertainties, it's easy to fixate on the problems rather than trusting in God's provision and guidance.

2. Fear of the Unknown: Anxiety often arises from fear of the future and the unknown. This fear can overshadow the assurance of God's sovereignty and His plans for our lives.

3. Self-Reliance: Relying solely on our own strength and understanding can lead to anxiety, as we feel the weight of responsibility without leaning on God's wisdom and provision.

Biblical Encouragement and Practical Steps to Combat Anxiety

- 63 -

1. Prayer: Turn worries into prayers, casting all anxieties on God who cares for you (1 Peter 5:7). Pray for God's peace to guard your heart and mind (Philippians 4:6-7).

2. Scripture Memorization: Hide God's promises in your heart by memorizing verses that speak to His love, faithfulness, and provision (e.g., Isaiah 41:10; Psalm 56:3).

3. Community Support: Surround yourself with fellow believers who can offer encouragement, prayer, and support during times of anxiety (Hebrews 10:24-25).

4. Mindfulness of God's Presence: Practice mindfulness of God's presence throughout your day. Reflect on His love and faithfulness, intentionally focusing your thoughts on His praise over you (Psalm 139:17-18).

5. Seeking Professional Help: If anxiety persists and significantly impacts daily life, seek guidance from a trusted pastor or counselor who can provide biblical counsel and practical strategies for managing anxiety.

By anchoring ourselves in the truth of God's praise and love, we can confront worry and anxiety with faith and assurance. Through prayer, scripture, community, and mindfulness of God's presence, we can experience His peace that surpasses all understanding (Philippians 4:7) and find strength to navigate life's challenges with confidence in His steadfast love.

Living in the Light of God's Praise

Encouragement to Live Confidently

Understanding that God rejoices over us with singing empowers believers to live confidently and boldly. This truth reveals the depth of God's love and affirmation, which transcends circumstances and challenges. Here's how you can encourage readers to embrace this perspective:

1. Identity in God's Love: Remind readers that their identity is rooted in God's unwavering love and acceptance. They are valued and cherished by the Creator of the universe.

2. Confidence in Decision-Making: Knowing that God delights in His people gives confidence in making decisions. Seek His guidance and trust that He rejoices over each step taken in alignment with His will.

3. Courage in Challenges: Face challenges with courage, knowing that God's praise over us signifies His presence and support. His joy strengthens us to persevere through difficulties.

Impact on Daily Life and Decision-Making

Living in the light of God's praise transforms daily life and decision-making in profound ways:

- ❖ **Assurance and Peace:** Believers experience a deep sense of assurance and peace, even amidst uncertainties, knowing that God delights in them.
- ❖ **Clarity in Priorities:** Understanding God's praise helps clarify priorities, focusing on eternal values rather than temporary concerns.
- ❖ **Boldness in Faith:** It fosters boldness in faith, encouraging believers to step out in obedience to God's calling and promises.

Testimonies and Examples

- ❖ **David:** Despite his flaws, David experienced God's joy and favor, exemplified in his psalms of praise and worship (Psalm 18:19-20).
- ❖ **Paul and Silas:** While imprisoned, they sang hymns to God, demonstrating faith and trust amidst adversity (Acts 16:25).
- ❖ **Modern Examples:** Many believers today testify to living confidently in God's praise, sharing how this truth has shaped their resilience, faithfulness, and joy in serving God.

Conclusion

Living in the light of God's praise invites believers into a transformative relationship where they find security, courage, and purpose. Embrace God's delight in you as a constant source of strength and motivation in daily life. Allow His joy to permeate your decisions and actions, knowing that you are deeply loved and celebrated by the Almighty God. As you live out this truth, may it inspire others to seek and experience the profound joy of living in God's presence and purpose.

When you understand this truth, it provides a deeper sense of peace and joy. There is no reason to be shaken or waver through thoughts or feelings of discouragement. God has you! He is proud of you. He helps to order every single step you take, if we take the time to hear His whispers.

Chapter Five

——— · ★ · ———

No Weapon...

Introduction

Innate peace and contentment transcend into joy when you aware of God' s Word and promises. One of them being "no weapon formed against you will prosper, as it reads in Isaiah 54:17.

The Bible says "No weapon formed against you shall prosper, and every tongue which rises against you in judgment you shall be condemned. This is the heritage of the servants of the Lord, and their righteousness is from Me," says the Lord.

These words from Isaiah offer a profound assurance that God's protection extends to His servants, guarding them against any weapon or accusation aimed at their downfall. They stand as a testament to God's sovereignty and faithfulness in defending His people's righteousness, ensuring that His purposes prevail despite the challenges they face.

Throughout this chapter, we will explore the depth of this promise, the direct connection for daily living, and drawing inspiration from testimonies of those who have experienced God's protective hand in their lives. As we unpack Isaiah 54:17, let us be reminded of God's enduring promise to shield and uphold His faithful servants, empowering them to walk in confidence and victory.

Verse Analysis: Isaiah 54:17

The text of Isaiah 54:17 reads -

"No weapon formed against you shall prosper, and every tongue which rises against you in judgment you shall condemn. This is the heritage of the servants of the Lord, and their righteousness is from Me," says the Lord.

Isaiah 54:17 conveys a powerful message of divine protection and assurance for believers. Let's break down its meaning:

1. No Weapon Formed Against You Shall Prosper: This phrase assures believers that any weapon or scheme devised against them will ultimately fail. It emphasizes God's sovereignty over adversity and His ability to thwart the plans of those who oppose His people (Psalm 37:23-24).

2. Every Tongue which Rises Against You in Judgment You Shall Condemn: This part assures believers that accusations or judgments spoken against them will not prevail. It reflects God's promise to vindicate His people and silence false accusations (Isaiah 50:8-9).

3. This is the Heritage of the Servants of the Lord: The promise of protection and vindication is not just a temporary blessing but a heritage passed down to all who serve and follow the Lord faithfully. It speaks to the enduring covenant relationship between God and His people, not for a day, week, or season, but for a lifetime!

4. Their Righteousness is from Me, Says the Lord: God affirms that the righteousness of His servants does not come from their own efforts but is imputed to them by Him. It underscores the divine origin of righteousness and the assurance of God's favor upon those who walk uprightly before Him (Philippians 3:9).

Context within the Book of Isaiah

Isaiah 54:17 is situated within the broader context of Isaiah's prophetic message to Israel. In chapters 40-66, often referred to as Deutero-Isaiah or Second Isaiah, the prophet addresses the restoration and future glory of God's people after the exile. This section emphasizes God's faithfulness, His redemptive plans for His people, and His promise to establish a new covenant with them.

Specifically, chapter 54 celebrates the future restoration of Jerusalem and portrays God as a compassionate husband who restores His covenant relationship with His people. The imagery of barrenness is transformed into fruitfulness (Isaiah 54:1-3) and the assurance of divine protection (Isaiah 54:15-17) are central themes. Isaiah 54:17, therefore, serves as a climactic affirmation of God's enduring covenant and protection over His chosen ones amidst opposition and adversity.

Life is not always smooth sailing. Alongside the ups and downs, you are sure to encounter from time to time, people who are not for you or a situation that makes you uncomfortable or puts you in harms way. I've learned to call on Jesus in challenging times. Literally, calling His name, "Jesus" can stop a car from swerving into you on the road, and offers protection, whether needed for your mind, body, and spirit.

God's promise of protection for believers is a cornerstone of faith, rooted in His character of love, sovereignty, and faithfulness. Throughout Scripture, we find numerous assurances that God watches over His people and shields them from harm:

1. Psalm 91:1-2, 4: "He who dwells in the shelter of the Most High will abide in the shadow of the Almighty. I will say to the Lord, 'My refuge and my fortress, my God, in whom I trust.'... He will cover you with his pinions, and under his wings you will find refuge; his faithfulness is a shield and buckler."

2. Psalm 121:7-8: "The Lord will keep you from all evil; he will keep your life. The Lord will keep your going out and your coming in from this time forth and forevermore."

3. Isaiah 41:10: "Fear not, for I am with you; be not dismayed, for I am your God; I will strengthen you, I will help you, I will uphold you with my righteous right hand."

Examples from Scripture

- ❖ **Daniel in the Lions' Den (Daniel 6):** God protected Daniel from the mouths of lions when he was unjustly accused and thrown into the den.

- ❖ **The Exodus from Egypt (Exodus 14):** God parted the Red Sea to rescue the Israelites from Pharaoh's pursuing army, demonstrating His power over natural forces and His commitment to deliver His people.

- ❖ **David and Goliath (1 Samuel 17):** God enabled David to defeat the giant Goliath, showcasing His strength and protection over His chosen servant.

Relating to Isaiah 54:17

Isaiah 54:17 addresses by promising protection against "weapons" formed against believers. These weapons can include spiritual attacks such as doubt, temptation, persecution, and spiritual oppression aimed at undermining faith and hindering God's purposes in our lives, or physical occurrences.

Standing Firm in Faith

Believers can stand firm in spiritual warfare by:

❖ **Putting on the Armor of God:** Ephesians 6:10-18 instructs believers to wear the armor of God, including the belt of truth, the breastplate of righteousness, the shield of faith, the helmet of salvation, and the sword of the Spirit (the Word of God).

❖ **Prayer and Dependence on God:** Regular prayer, communion with God, and reliance on His strength are crucial in resisting spiritual attacks (James 4:7-8).

❖ **Studying Scripture:** Knowing and applying God's Word helps believers discern truth from deception and equips them to combat spiritual falsehoods (Hebrews 4:12).

In conclusion, God's promise of protection assures believers of His constant vigilance and care amidst spiritual warfare. By trusting in His promises, putting on spiritual armor, and standing firm in faith, believers can overcome spiritual attacks and live victoriously in Christ.

Living in Confidence

Living Confidently in God's Protection

God promises to repay you double for any trouble you have gone through (Isaiah 61:7). So there is much reason to rejoice in gladness if you may be walking through a challenging season. You will always certainly come out better • increased joy, peace, love, and/or resources.

Deep roots of faith don't fear strong winds. When you have deep roots grounded in God's truth, you can't help but to live in peace and joy, no matter the circumstance. Living confidently in the assurance of God's protection is both a privilege and a necessity for every believer. People who live in confidence of God's promise of protection, exhibit immense joy, grounded in peace and comfort. Here are some ways to cultivate and sustain this confidence:

1. Anchor Yourself in Scripture: Regularly study and meditate on passages that affirm God's promises of protection and provision (Psalm 23, Psalm 91, Isaiah 41:10). Allow God's Word to shape your perspective and strengthen your faith.

2. Prayer and Communion with God: Develop a consistent prayer life where you express your fears, concerns, and gratitude to God. Through prayer, seek His guidance, provision, and protection in every aspect of your life (Philippians 4:6-7).

3. Reflect on Past Experiences: Recall moments when God intervened or protected you in unexpected ways. Reflecting on these experiences reinforces your trust in His faithfulness and strengthens your confidence in His ongoing care.

4. Surround Yourself with Faith-filled Community: Engage with fellow believers who encourage and support your faith journey. Sharing testimonies and praying together builds a sense of unity and reinforces trust in God's promises (Hebrews 10:24-25).

5. Strive to follow the Guidance: None of us are perfect, however the Bible provides a solid foundation for living good and well. Doing right by others, living in peace, and knowing that God is our banner and directs are steps, allows us to live confidently.

Practical Ways to Strengthen Faith and Trust

- ❖ **Daily Devotions:** Set aside time each day for personal devotions, including reading Scripture, prayer, and reflection.
- ❖ **Journaling:** Keep a prayer journal or gratitude journal to document answered prayers and moments of God's provision and protection.
- ❖ **Community of Believers:** Attend church services, join small groups, or participate in Bible studies to deepen your understanding of God's Word and receive encouragement from others.

Reflect on times in your life when you've been protected. Was it from a car accident, potentially destructive relationship, or extra provision financially?

In conclusion, living in confidence in God's protection involves nurturing a deep faith through Scripture, prayer, community, and reflection on God's faithfulness in both biblical accounts and personal testimonies. By strengthening your faith and trusting in God's promises, you can navigate life's challenges with assurance and experience His ongoing protection and provision.

Chapter Six

Your Shield

Introduction

Just as God promised us that no weapon formed against us will prosper, it is paramount to know that He is also your shield and your banner. Because we are human, in the journey of life, it is inevitable that we will encounter situations that natural stir up anxiety, fear and uncertainty within us. These moments can challenge our faith and shake our confidence.

Yet, as believers, we have a profound assurance: God is our shield and protector, guiding and safeguarding us through every step. You may be asking yourself - what does this have to do with being happy or joyful? It points out that if we are truly walling in a spirit of joy, which stems from understanding the peace of God, His promises, and covering, When you exhibit happy characteristics, it's easier to waver between your thoughts and feelings, exhibiting unsteady behavior.

The Bible is enamored with imagery and affirmations of God as a shield, emphasizing His commitment to protect, cover, and defend His people. Psalm 3:3 declares, "But you, Lord, are a shield around me, my glory, the One who lifts my head high." This verse captures the essence of God's protective nature, surrounding us with His presence and lifting us above our fears, empowering us and providing confidence in our every move.

Similarly, Psalm 28:7 affirms, "The Lord is my strength and my shield; my heart trusts in him, and he helps me." These words remind us that our strength is not in our circumstances but in the unwavering protection of our God. He is both our shield and our strength, providing the support and defense we need to face life's challenges.

As we explore this chapter, we will uncover the significance of God as our shield, understand how this metaphor translates into our daily lives, and learn to live with the confidence that comes from His divine protection. Through scriptural insights, personal stories, and practical applications, we will embrace the truth that with God as our shield, there is no need to fear.

The Concept of God as a Shield

Explaining the Biblical Imagery of God as a Shield

In the Bible, the imagery of God as a shield is a powerful and recurring theme that underscores His role as our protector and defender. This metaphor is vividly portrayed in numerous scriptures, highlighting God's commitment to safeguarding His people from harm.

1. Psalm 18:2: "The Lord is my rock, my fortress and my deliverer; my God is my rock, in whom I take refuge, my shield and the horn of my salvation, my stronghold."

2. Psalm 84:11: "For the Lord God is a sun and shield; the Lord bestows favor and honor; no good thing does he withhold from those whose walk is blameless."

3. Proverbs 30:5: "Every word of God is flawless; he is a shield to those who take refuge in him."

These verses emphasize that God not only provides protection but also offers refuge and strength. The imagery of a shield suggests a barrier that intercepts and deflects attacks, ensuring the safety of the one behind it. This protective aspect of God's nature is a source of immense comfort and security for believers.

Key Functions of a Shield

1. Protection: The primary function of a shield was to protect the warrior from physical harm. By holding the shield, soldiers could block or deflect blows, minimizing injury.

2. Defensive Strategy: Shields were used in various formations, such as the phalanx, where soldiers stood close together, their shields overlapping to create a nearly impenetrable barrier.

3. Psychological Assurance: Holding a shield gave soldiers a sense of security and confidence, knowing they had a reliable means of defense against the enemy's assaults.

Metaphorical Application in Spiritual Life

In the same way that a physical shield protects a soldier, God acts as a spiritual shield for believers. This metaphor extends beyond physical protection to encompass emotional, mental, and spiritual security.

1. Spiritual Defense: Just as a shield guards against physical attacks, God shields us from spiritual attacks. This includes protection from doubt, fear, temptation, and the schemes of the enemy. Ephesians 6:16 speaks of the "shield of faith" that can extinguish all the flaming arrows of the evil one.

2. Emotional and Mental Security: God's protection offers peace of mind and heart. Knowing that He is our shield allows us to face life's challenges without succumbing to anxiety or despair. Philippians 4:7 promises that the peace of God, which transcends all understanding, will guard our hearts and minds in Christ Jesus.

3. Guidance, Comfort, and Refuge: A shield also symbolizes a place of comfort. In times of trouble, we can take shelter in God's presence, knowing that He is our fortress and safe haven. Psalm 46:1-2 affirms that "God is our refuge and strength, an ever-present help in trouble. Therefore we will not fear..."

4. Confidence and Strength: Understanding God as our shield empowers us to live boldly and confidently. We can move forward in life with the assurance that He is always protecting and guiding us, much like a soldier who advances in battle with a shield.

Scriptural Foundations

Psalm 3:3: "But you, Lord, are a shield around me, my glory, the One who lifts my head high."

This verse portrays God as an encompassing shield, not merely protecting from the front but surrounding the believer entirely. It highlights God's comprehensive protection and His role in restoring dignity and hope. When life's challenges weigh us down, God not only shields us but also lifts our heads, instilling confidence and courage.

Psalm 28:7: "The Lord is my strength and my shield; my heart trusts in him, and he helps me."

Here, the psalmist acknowledges God as both a source of strength and a shield. Trusting in God results in divine assistance and support. This verse emphasizes the relational aspect of faith, where trust in God activates His protective and strengthening presence in our lives.

Ephesians 6:16: "In addition to all this, take up the shield of faith, with which you can extinguish all the flaming arrows of the evil one."

The Apostle Paul, in his letter to the Ephesians, speaks of the shield of faith as part of the armor of God. This shield is unique because it is not made of physical materials but of faith itself. It has the power to extinguish the "flaming arrows" of doubt, fear, and temptation that the enemy launches. This metaphor emphasizes the active role of faith in spiritual defense.

No Need to Fear: Exploring Common Fears and Anxieties

In today's world, people face numerous fears and anxieties, such as:

1. Fear of Failure: Concerns about not meeting expectations or achieving goals.

2. Fear of Rejection: Worries about being unloved or unaccepted by others.

3. Fear of the Unknown: Anxiety about uncertain futures and unforeseen events.

4. Fear of Loss: Dread of losing loved ones, possessions, or status.

5. Fear of Illness or Death: Apprehensions about health and mortality.

These fears can paralyze individuals, preventing them from living fully and confidently. They can lead to stress, anxiety disorders, and a sense of hopelessness.

Recognizing God as our shield brings a profound sense of peace and security:

1. Divine Protection: Knowing that God is our shield reassures us that we are protected from both seen and unseen dangers. His protection is not limited by time or space, offering constant vigilance over our lives.

2. Strength and Courage: As our shield, God provides the strength we need to face challenges. His presence emboldens us, allowing us to confront fears with confidence.

3. Trust and Dependence: Trusting in God as our shield shifts our focus from our fears to His power. This dependence on Him alleviates the burden of trying to control everything ourselves.

4. Peace of Mind: The assurance that God is shielding us from harm brings peace that transcends our understanding, reducing anxiety and promoting mental well-being.

God Holds Your Every Footstep

- 83 -

Explaining the Idea That God Guides and Secures Our Paths

The notion that God holds our every footstep is a profound expression of His active involvement in our lives. It conveys the understanding that God not only observes our journey but also guides, supports, and secures our steps. This divine guidance is a promise of both direction and stability, ensuring that we do not walk alone but are accompanied by God's wisdom and care.

Proverbs 3:5-6: "Trust in the Lord with all your heart and lean not on your own understanding; in all your ways submit to him, and he will make your paths straight." This scripture emphasizes the importance of trusting God fully and not relying solely on our own wisdom. By submitting our ways to Him, we allow God to direct our paths, ensuring that we navigate life according to His perfect will. This submission is a blend of humility and faith, acknowledging that God's understanding surpasses our own.

Psalm 37:23-24: "The Lord makes firm the steps of the one who delights in him; though he may stumble, he will not fall, for the Lord upholds him with his hand." Here, the psalmist describes how God establishes and supports the steps of those who take pleasure in Him. Even when we encounter difficulties and stumble, God's hand sustains us, preventing us from falling completely. This imagery of divine support highlights God's commitment to our stability and well-being.

Practical Implications of Trusting God with Our Daily Steps and Decisions

1. Decision-Making with Confidence: When we trust that God holds our every footstep, we can approach decision-making with greater confidence. By seeking His guidance through prayer and scripture, we align our choices with His will, reducing anxiety about the outcomes. Knowing that God directs our paths allows us to move forward without fear of making the wrong decisions.

2. Navigating Uncertainty: Life is filled with uncertainties and unforeseen challenges. Trusting in God's guidance means believing that He is with us even in the unknown. Proverbs 3:5-6 encourages us to rely not on our understanding but on God's wisdom. This trust becomes a source of peace, enabling us to face uncertainty with a calm assurance that God is in control.

3. Personal Growth and Development: When we allow God to guide our steps, we open ourselves to personal growth and transformation. God's direction often leads us to experiences and lessons that shape our character and deepen our faith. By trusting His plan, we embrace growth opportunities that we might otherwise avoid out of fear or uncertainty.

4. Overcoming Obstacles: Psalm 37:23-24 reassures us that even when we stumble, we will not fall, for God upholds us. This means that setbacks and obstacles are not the end but part of the journey. With God's support, we can overcome challenges and continue moving forward, learning and growing from each experience.

5. Daily Dependence on God: Trusting God with our steps is a daily exercise of faith. It involves continuously seeking His will through prayer, reading the Bible, and being attentive to the Holy Spirit's promptings. This daily dependence fosters a closer relationship with God, as we learn to walk in step with Him, trusting His direction in both small and significant matters.

6. Testimonies of Divine Guidance: Real-life examples of individuals who trusted God with their steps can be incredibly inspiring. Consider the story of a person who felt called to change careers despite uncertainties. By trusting God's guidance, they navigated the transition successfully and found fulfillment in their new path. Such testimonies reinforce the truth that God's guidance leads to purposeful and fulfilling outcomes.

Practical Steps to Embrace God's Protection

Embracing God's protection involves more than just believing in it; it requires actively trusting and seeking His presence in our daily lives. Here are practical steps to help readers incorporate this trust into their everyday routine:

Daily Prayer and Meditation

Spending Time in Prayer to Seek God's Guidance and Protection

1. Start the Day with Prayer: Begin each day with a prayer asking for God's guidance, protection, and wisdom. This sets a positive and focused tone for the day.

2. Meditate on God's Promises: Take time to meditate on the promises of God's protection found in the Bible. Reflect on how these promises apply to your current circumstances.

3. Express Gratitude: Thank God for His continuous protection and for the ways He has safeguarded you in the past. Gratitude strengthens faith and reinforces trust in His ongoing care.

Scripture Memorization

Learning and Recalling Verses About God's Protection

1. Select Key Verses: Choose a few key verses that speak about God's protection, such as Psalm 91:4, "He will cover you with his feathers, and under his wings you will find refuge; his faithfulness will be your shield and rampart."

2. Regular Review: Set aside time each day to read and memorize these verses. Repetition will help internalize these truths.

3. Use Memory Aids: Utilize tools like flashcards, apps, or writing verses in a journal to aid memorization.

4. Apply Verses to Daily Life: When facing challenges or fears, recall these verses to remind yourself of God's promises. Let them guide your thoughts and actions.

Engaging with a Faith Community for Encouragement and Support

1. Join a Faith Group: Participate in a small group, Bible study, or church community where you can share experiences and receive support.

2. Share Testimonies: Listen to and share testimonies of God's protection. Hearing how God has worked in others' lives can be a powerful encouragement.

3. Pray Together: Engage in group prayer sessions. Praying with others can strengthen your faith and provide a sense of solidarity.

4. Offer Support: Be an active part of the community by offering support to others. Encouraging others in their faith journey reinforces your own trust in God's protection.

Implementing These Steps

To make these practices a consistent part of your life, consider creating a routine or schedule:

- ❖ **Morning Routine:** Start your day with prayer and a brief meditation on scripture.
- ❖ **Daily Breaks:** Take short breaks throughout the day to recite memorized verses or pray.
- ❖ **Evening Reflection:** End your day with reflection, gratitude, and prayer, recounting how you experienced God's protection throughout the day.
- ❖ **Weekly Community Engagement:** Dedicate a specific time each week to participate in a faith community activity.

By integrating these practical steps into your daily life, you can cultivate a deeper sense of God's protection and presence. Trusting in God's guidance and care will become a natural and integral part of your everyday experience, providing peace and confidence as you navigate life's challenges.

Benefits of Embracing God's Protection

Embracing God's protection through these practical steps brings about numerous spiritual, emotional, and relational benefits:

Spiritual Benefits

1. Strengthened Faith: Regular prayer, meditation, and scripture memorization deepen your relationship with God and bolster your faith in His promises.

2. Increased Spiritual Discernment: By seeking God's guidance daily, you become more attuned to His will and direction, making it easier to navigate life's decisions with clarity and confidence.

3. Inner Peace: Knowing that God is your shield and protector alleviates fear and anxiety, replacing them with a profound sense of peace and security.

Emotional Benefits

1. Reduced Anxiety: Trusting in God's protection can significantly reduce worries and anxieties about the future, providing emotional stability and resilience.

2. Enhanced Emotional Well-being: Gratitude and reflection on God's faithfulness lead to a more positive outlook on life, improving overall emotional health.

3. Increased Resilience: Regularly reminding yourself of God's promises helps build emotional resilience, enabling you to face challenges with courage and hope.

Relational Benefits

1. Stronger Community Bonds: Engaging with a faith community fosters meaningful relationships, providing a network of support and encouragement.

2. Mutual Encouragement: Sharing experiences and testimonies within the community reinforces collective faith and inspires others to trust in God's protection.

3. Greater Compassion: As you grow in your understanding of God's love and protection, you become more empathetic and supportive towards others, enhancing your relational interactions.

Chapter Seven

Are You a Giver?

Introduction

Serving others giving of my time and resources provides a sense of immeasurable joy! Regardless of whether you are a believer or not, there is a sound principle in what you give out, you get back to you. When you give selflessly to others and the world, it comes back to you, and often times, multiple times more what you gave; whether in time or resources.

In a world often driven by self-interest and individual success, the timeless virtue of generosity stands as a beacon of hope and transformation. At the heart of this chapter lies a fundamental truth: by giving of ourselves—our time, talents, resources, our love and support—we not only enrich the lives of those around us but also experience deep fulfillment and joy in our own lives.

The biblical principle of generosity is woven throughout Scripture, offering us a roadmap for living a life that mirrors God's boundless love and compassion. Proverbs 11:25 declares, "A generous person will prosper; whoever refreshes others will be refreshed."

This verse encapsulates the reciprocal nature of generosity when we pour out blessings onto others, we too are blessed in return. Acts 20:35 echoes this sentiment, reminding us of Jesus' words, "It is more blessed to give than to receive." These passages highlight that the act of giving is not just about meeting needs but also about cultivating a spirit of selflessness and grace that transforms both the giver and the receiver.

As we explore this theme, we will uncover the multifaceted ways in which giving can shape lives and communities. Generosity is not confined to financial contributions; it encompasses acts of service, mentorship, encouragement, and the simple yet powerful gift of presence. When we invest in people, we sow seeds of hope, inspire growth, and foster connections that form the foundation of strong, supportive communities.

Through this chapter, we aim to illuminate the transformative power of generosity and provide practical insights into how we can all become more intentional givers. By looking at the examples set forth in the Bible and sharing contemporary stories of lives changed through acts of giving, we will see how each of us holds the potential to make a significant impact.

The Principle of Generosity

Biblical Foundations:

Generosity is a core virtue that finds its roots deeply embedded in the teachings of the Bible. Throughout Scripture, we encounter numerous passages that underscore the transformative power of giving and its profound impact on both the giver and the receiver.

Key Scriptures:

1. Proverbs 11:25 - "A generous person will prosper; whoever refreshes others will be refreshed."

- ❖ This proverb highlights the reciprocal nature of generosity. Those who freely give of themselves, whether in material resources, kindness, or support, are themselves enriched and revitalized. It speaks to the spiritual principle that generosity breeds blessings and abundance.

2. Acts 20:35 - **"It is more blessed to give than to receive."**

- ❖ These words, attributed to Jesus Himself, remind us of the inherent joy and blessing found in acts of giving. Beyond mere material benefits, giving cultivates a spirit of humility, compassion, and selflessness, aligning our hearts with God's abundant grace and love.

Teachings of Jesus:

Jesus Christ, through His life and teachings, exemplified the principle of generosity in profound ways:

1. The Parable of the Good Samaritan (Luke 10:25-37):

In this parable, Jesus illustrates the essence of loving one's neighbor through the selfless actions of a Samaritan who helps a wounded stranger. The Samaritan demonstrates compassion and generosity by sacrificially caring for someone in need, regardless of cultural or religious differences. This parable challenges us to extend kindness and support to all people, regardless of social status or background.

2. The Principle of Sowing and Reaping (Luke 6:38):

Jesus teaches, "Give, and it will be given to you. A good measure, pressed down, shaken together and running over, will be poured into your lap. For with the measure you use, it will be measured to you."

This principle emphasizes that the manner in which we give—whether in generosity of spirit, resources, or love—will determine the abundance of blessings we receive in return. It encourages us to give freely and generously, trusting in God's provision and the law of spiritual harvest.

Understanding and practicing the principle of generosity not only blesses others but also enriches our own lives. It fosters a spirit of gratitude, humility, and solidarity within communities, promoting mutual care and support.

As we reflect on these foundational scriptures and teachings, we are called to embrace generosity as a fundamental expression of our faith and love for God and others. By following the example set by Jesus and heeding the wisdom of Scripture, we can cultivate a lifestyle characterized by compassion, grace, and abundant blessings for all.

The Ripple Effect of Generosity

Transforming Lives:

Generosity has a profound capacity to transform individual lives, often sparking a ripple effect that extends far beyond the initial act of giving.

Highlighting the Far-Reaching Impact:

Generosity sets off a chain reaction of positive outcomes, demonstrating how a single act of kindness can inspire others to give and create lasting change:

Building Strong Communities:

When generosity becomes a cultural norm within a community, it fosters resilience, cooperation, and mutual support:

❖ **Support Networks:** Communities that prioritize generosity develop robust support networks where individuals and families feel empowered to seek and offer help without stigma or judgment.

❖ **Economic Stability:** Collective efforts in giving contribute to economic stability by addressing immediate needs and promoting sustainable development initiatives.

Examples of Thriving Communities:

1. Neighborly Support: In a suburban neighborhood, residents organize regular volunteer days to assist elderly homeowners with household repairs and maintenance. This collaborative effort strengthens neighborhood bonds and improves overall quality of life.

2. Community Gardens: Urban communities cultivate shared gardens where residents grow fresh produce together. These initiatives not only promote healthy eating but also build relationships and reduce food insecurity.

Practical Steps to Become a Giver

Assess Your Time, Resources, and Emotional Capacity:

1. Evaluate Your Resources: Take stock of your time, talents, and finances to understand how you can contribute effectively.

Consider what you have to offer and how you can best utilize these resources for the benefit of others.

2. Allocate Giving: Set aside a specific portion of your income or time dedicated to acts of generosity. This intentional allocation ensures that giving becomes a regular and prioritized part of your life.

Start Small and Be Consistent:

1. Embrace Small Acts: Understand that generosity doesn't always require grand gestures. Small, consistent acts of kindness can have a profound impact on individuals and communities. Examples include offering a listening ear to a friend in need, mentoring, writing an encouraging note, or performing random acts of kindness like paying for someone's meal.

2. Consistency Matters: Make giving a habit by incorporating it into your daily routine. Whether it's a weekly commitment to volunteer at a local shelter or a monthly donation to a charitable organization, consistency builds momentum and reinforces the joy of giving.

Engage with Your Community:

1. Join Community Initiatives: Get involved in local clubs, organizations, or church groups that prioritize service and support. These groups often provide opportunities to connect with like-minded individuals and contribute to meaningful causes together.

2. Identify Local Needs: Look for ways to address specific needs within your community. Whether it's organizing a neighborhood cleanup, participating in a fundraiser for a local school, or volunteering at a community garden, your involvement can make a tangible difference.

Conclusion:

By assessing your resources, starting small with consistent acts of kindness, and actively engaging with your community, you can cultivate a lifestyle of generosity that enriches both your life and the lives of others. Remember, every act of giving, no matter how small, contributes to building stronger, more compassionate communities where everyone thrives. Take the first step today and discover the profound joy and fulfillment that comes from being a giver.

Chapter Eight

Relax & Take a Vacation

Introduction

In today's fast-paced world, creating a joyful and peaceful environment is essential for maintaining a and mindset is a necessity for personal well-being and healthy relationships. Our outlook on life profoundly influences how we experience and interact with the world around us. A positive attitude can enhance resilience, foster stronger connections with others, and contribute to overall happiness and satisfaction.

Importance of a Joyful and Peaceful Environment

An optimistic attitude serves as a powerful tool for navigating life's challenges with grace and optimism. It allows us to approach difficulties with a solution-oriented mindset, seeking opportunities for growth rather than dwelling on setbacks. This mindset not only boosts our mental and emotional resilience but also enables us to inspire and uplift those around us.

In a season where you are actively trying to change and maintain your environment to thrive in peace and joy, be very mindful of anyone of anything that may distract progress.

Mindset Check

Identifying Signs of a Negative Mindset & Encouraging Self-Reflection:

Self-reflection is key to understanding and changing one's mindset. It involves:

- ❖ **Awareness of Thoughts:** Pay attention to your inner dialogue and how it influences your emotions and actions.
- ❖ **Recognizing Patterns:** Identify recurring negative thoughts or behaviors that may contribute to a pessimistic outlook.
- ❖ **Choosing Perspective:** Practice viewing challenges as opportunities for growth and learning, shifting from a reactive to a proactive mindset.

Have Fun!

Emphasizing the Importance of Enjoying Life:

Finding joy and pleasure in life is essential for mental and emotional well-being:

- ❖ **Leisure and Relaxation:** Engaging in hobbies, spending time with loved ones, or simply taking time for oneself can recharge and rejuvenate the mind.

- ❖ **Benefits of Leisure Time:** Relaxation fosters creativity, reduces stress levels, and improves overall happiness. It allows for a balanced life where work and responsibilities are complemented by enjoyable activities.

Work-Life Balance and Harmony

Avoiding Work-Related Negativity Outside of Work:

1. Maintaining Boundaries: It's important to set boundaries between work and personal life. Avoid discussing work-related negatives or challenges extensively outside of the workplace. Constantly bringing work stress or issues into personal interactions can hinder relaxation and strain relationships.

2. Creating Positive Spaces: Designate certain times or places where work-related topics are off-limits. This allows for more meaningful connections and enjoyment of leisure time without the weight of work-related stressors.

Embracing Time for Relaxation and Rejuvenation

1.Intentional Time Off: Encourage individuals to view vacation time as essential for recharging and rejuvenating. It's an opportunity to unwind, refresh the mind, and reconnect with oneself and loved ones.

2. Disconnecting from Work: Advocate for fully disconnecting from work responsibilities during vacations. This includes refraining from checking work emails or taking work-related calls unless absolutely necessary. By disconnecting, individuals can fully immerse themselves in relaxation and leisure activities.

3. Benefits of Relaxation: Emphasize the positive impact of relaxation on overall well-being. Taking breaks from work allows for better focus and productivity upon returning, reduces stress levels, and improves overall mental and emotional health. By maintaining boundaries between work and personal life and fully embracing vacation time for relaxation and rejuvenation, individuals can achieve a healthier work-life balance. This approach not only enhances personal well-being but also fosters stronger relationships and greater enjoyment of leisure activities.

Singing and Expression

Therapeutic Benefits of Singing and Self-Expression:

1. Emotional Release: Singing allows for the expression of emotions that may be difficult to articulate verbally. It serves as a cathartic outlet for stress, sadness, joy, or any other feelings one may experience.

2. Mind-Body Connection: Engaging in singing activates areas of the brain associated with pleasure and reward, releasing endorphins that contribute to a sense of well-being and relaxation.

3. Stress Reduction: Singing has been shown to lower cortisol levels, the hormone associated with stress. It can promote relaxation and reduce anxiety, providing a natural form of stress relief.

4. Improvement in Mood: The act of singing can elevate mood by boosting serotonin levels in the brain, which helps regulate mood and social behavior.

Encouraging Freedom of Self-Expression:

1. Overcoming Inhibitions: Many people feel self-conscious about singing or expressing themselves openly. Encourage readers to embrace their unique voice and talents without fear of judgment or criticism.

2. Building Confidence: Regularly engaging in singing and self-expression can enhance self-esteem and confidence. It fosters a sense of empowerment and authenticity in one's identity.

3. Creating Connection: Singing together with others, whether in a choir, community group, or even with friends and family, fosters a sense of belonging and connection. It strengthens social bonds and promotes unity.

4. Exploring Creativity: Self-expression through singing allows individuals to explore their creativity and artistic abilities. It encourages exploration of different musical genres, styles, and forms of expression.

Chapter Nine

Watch Your Words - The Power of Life and Death

Introduction

Words hold immense power beyond mere communication; they have the ability to shape reality, influence emotions, and impact relationships. The ancient wisdom that "life and death are in the power of the tongue" underscores this profound truth. Every word spoken carries weight, capable of either building up or tearing down.

In this chapter, we delve into the transformative power of words, urging mindfulness in how we speak. Our words not only reflect our inner thoughts and beliefs but also have a tangible effect on our surroundings. Whether in personal interactions, professional settings, or even in our private thoughts, the words we choose can create pathways to success or sow seeds of discord.

The Power of Words

Biblical and Philosophical Perspectives:

Words have long been recognized as having significant power in shaping reality and influencing outcomes. In various religious and philosophical traditions, the concept of spoken words carrying creative or destructive power is foundational. For instance, in the Christian tradition, Proverbs 18:21 states, "Death and life are in the power of the tongue, and those who love it will eat its fruits," highlighting the dual potential of words to bring either harm or healing.

From a philosophical standpoint, thinkers across cultures have emphasized the importance of speech in shaping thoughts, emotions, and societal structures. Plato's dialogues, for example, explore how rhetoric and persuasive speech can sway opinions and influence actions, underscoring the ethical responsibility that comes with speech.

Examples of Impactful Words

Throughout history and literature, numerous examples attest to the transformative power of words. Leaders such as Mahatma Gandhi, Martin Luther King Jr., and Nelson Mandela used their words to inspire movements and bring about social change. Conversely, instances of hate speech and propaganda have incited violence and division.

In personal relationships, positive affirmations and expressions of love have strengthened bonds and fostered growth, while harsh criticisms or hurtful remarks have caused emotional wounds and strained connections. These examples illustrate how words can either build up or tear down individuals, communities, and societies.

Speaking Life

Definition and Importance:

Speaking life into situations and relationships involves using words intentionally to encourage, uplift, and affirm. It goes beyond mere positivity; it encompasses fostering hope, inspiring confidence, and nurturing growth. When we speak life, we acknowledge the potential for positive outcomes and actively contribute to creating an environment conducive to flourishing.

Scriptural and Experiential Evidence:

Scriptures such as Ephesians 4:29 advise, "Let no corrupting talk come out of your mouths, but only such as is good for building up, as fits the occasion, that it may give grace to those who hear." This emphasizes the importance of using words to edify and empower rather than to tear down.

Stories abound of individuals whose lives have been transformed by words of encouragement and affirmation. From mentors who believed in their potential to friends who offered unwavering support, these examples demonstrate the profound impact of positive speech on personal development and well-being.

By understanding the power of speaking life, we are called to cultivate a habit of mindful and intentional communication. Through our words, we have the opportunity to create positive change, foster resilience in adversity, and build strong, supportive relationships.

Speaking Death

Definition and Consequences:

Negative speech, often referred to as "speaking death," encompasses words that criticize, condemn, discourage, or spread negativity. Such speech not only reflects a pessimistic mindset but also has detrimental effects on both individuals and relationships. When we speak death, we sow seeds of doubt, insecurity, and division.

Impact on Relationships and Self-Esteem:

Words of criticism can erode trust and create distance in relationships. Constant judgment or discouragement can undermine confidence and self-worth, leading to feelings of inadequacy or even depression. In personal and professional settings alike, negative speech can hinder growth, stifle creativity, and foster a toxic environment.

Manifestation of Words

Concept Exploration:

The concept of manifestation through speech posits that what we consistently speak about or affirm tends to manifest in our lives. This idea aligns with the principle that our words have creative power, influencing our thoughts, emotions, and actions. When we repeatedly speak positively or negatively about ourselves or our circumstances, we shape our reality accordingly.

Manifesting Positivity vs. Negativity:

Positive affirmations and declarations can cultivate a mindset of abundance, resilience, and optimism. By speaking positively about our goals, dreams, and relationships, we reinforce beliefs in our ability to achieve and attract positive outcomes.

Conversely, consistently dwelling on negative thoughts or verbalizing fears and doubts can reinforce feelings of hopelessness or failure. This negative self-talk can become a self-fulfilling prophecy, influencing behavior and outcomes in ways that align with our spoken beliefs.

Practical Application:

Understanding the manifestation of words invites us to practice mindfulness in our speech. By becoming aware of the words we use and their potential impact, we can intentionally choose to speak life, fostering positivity and empowerment in ourselves and others. This awareness also encourages us to challenge and replace negative speech patterns with affirming, constructive language, thereby promoting personal growth and cultivating healthier relationships.

Practical Tips for Positive Communication

1. Mindfulness in Daily Conversations:

- ❖ **Pause and Reflect:** Before speaking, take a moment to consider the impact of your words. Ask yourself if what you're about to say will build up or tear down.
- ❖ **Listen Actively:** Practice active listening to understand others' perspectives fully before responding. This reduces misunderstandings and promotes empathy.

2. Techniques for Speaking Life:

- ❖ **Use Encouraging Words:** Instead of criticizing, offer constructive feedback and encouragement. Focus on strengths and potential rather than shortcomings.
- ❖ **Affirm Others:** Express appreciation and admiration genuinely. Acknowledge efforts and achievements to uplift others' spirits.

3. Scriptural Guidance:

- ❖ **Proverbs 18:21:** "Death and life are in the power of the tongue, and those who love it will eat its fruits." This verse underscores the profound impact of our words on our lives and those around us. It reminds us to choose our words carefully, knowing they can either bring life or cause harm.

- ❖ **Ephesians 4:29:** "Let no corrupting talk come out of your mouths, but only such as is good for building up, as fits the occasion, that it may give grace to those who hear." This encourages us to speak words that edify and bring grace to others, fostering positive relationships and environments.

- ❖ **James 1:19:** "Know this, my beloved brothers: let every person be quick to hear, slow to speak, slow to anger." This verse advises us to prioritize listening over speaking hastily, promoting understanding and reducing conflict.

Application in Daily Life:

- ❖ **Prayer and Meditation:** Start and end your day with prayer or meditation, seeking guidance on your speech and interactions.

- ❖ **Accountability:** Surround yourself with friends or mentors who can help you monitor and improve your communication habits.

- ❖ **Practice Gratitude:** Cultivate a habit of gratitude, verbally acknowledging blessings and expressing appreciation for others regularly.

By integrating these practical tips and scriptural principles into daily life, we can nurture positive communication habits that build up others, strengthen relationships, and align with God's teachings on love and grace.

Chapter Ten

Give Thanks

Introduction

In the hustle and bustle of daily life, amidst challenges and triumphs, there exists a simple yet profound practice that has the power to transform our outlook and enrich our lives: gratitude. At its core, gratitude is more than a fleeting emotion; it is a deliberate and transformative habit that invites us to pause, reflect, and appreciate the blessings that surround us.

Imagine a day where, amidst the rush and routine, we take a moment to reflect on the moments that brought us joy, peace, or comfort. Whether it's a shared laugh with a friend, a beautiful sunrise on a morning commute, or a small act of kindness from a stranger, each of these moments holds within it an opportunity—to give thanks.

This chapter delves into the art of gratitude, encouraging us to cultivate a habit of reflection and appreciation. By exploring the concept of daily happiness and the power of gratitude, we embark on a journey to discover how this simple practice can bring about profound changes in our perspective, relationships, and overall well-being. Join me as we explore the transformative potential of giving thanks, one moment at a time.

Benefits of Gratitude

Gratitude, often considered a foundational virtue across cultures and philosophies, offers a multitude of benefits that extend far beyond mere politeness or manners. Here's a closer look at how practicing gratitude can significantly enhance our lives:

Psychological and Emotional Benefits:

- ❖ **Enhanced Positivity:** Gratitude helps shift our focus from what we lack to what we have, fostering a more optimistic outlook on life.
- ❖ **Reduced Stress:** Regular practice of gratitude has been linked to lower levels of stress and anxiety, promoting emotional resilience in the face of challenges.
- ❖ **Increased Happiness:** Studies have shown that grateful individuals tend to experience higher levels of happiness and life satisfaction, regardless of external circumstances.
- ❖ **Improved Mental Health:** Gratitude is associated with improved mental health outcomes, including reduced

symptoms of depression and greater overall psychological well-being.

Impact on Relationships and Overall Well-being:

1. Strengthened Relationships: Expressing gratitude cultivates a deeper sense of connection and appreciation in relationships, fostering trust and intimacy.

2. Generosity and Kindness: Grateful individuals are more likely to engage in prosocial behaviors, such as acts of kindness and generosity towards others.

3. Physical Health Benefits: Gratitude has been correlated with better physical health outcomes, including improved sleep quality, lower blood pressure, and a stronger immune system.

4. Resilience and Coping Skills: Gratitude helps build resilience by encouraging a focus on what is positive and meaningful, even in difficult times.

Scientific Perspective on Gratitude

Gratitude, once viewed primarily as a social courtesy, has garnered significant attention in scientific research for its profound effects on mental and physical well-being. Here's an exploration of how gratitude is supported by scientific findings:

Positive Effects of Gratitude:

1. Improved Mental Health: Research indicates that practicing gratitude can lead to reduced symptoms of depression and anxiety. Grateful individuals tend to have higher levels of positive emotions and lower levels of negative emotions.

2. Enhanced Emotional Regulation: Gratitude is associated with improved emotional resilience and the ability to cope with stress more effectively.

3. Physical Health Benefits: Studies have linked gratitude with better sleep quality, reduced inflammation, and improved cardiovascular health.

4. Stronger Relationships: Gratitude fosters a sense of connection and empathy, enhancing relationship satisfaction and social interactions.

Rewiring the Brain for Positivity:

1. Neurological Impact: Neuroscientific studies suggest that gratitude activates areas of the brain associated with reward, empathy, and emotional processing, such as the hypothalamus and ventral tegmental area.

2. Formation of New Habits: Regular practice of gratitude can lead to neuroplastic changes in the brain, reinforcing positive thought patterns and reducing the neural pathways of negativity.

Biblical Perspective on Gratitude

Gratitude holds a central place in many religious traditions, including Christianity, where it is seen as a spiritual practice that aligns with faith and spiritual growth:

Spiritual Growth and Faith:

1. Gratitude as Worship: In biblical teachings, gratitude is often presented as a form of worship and acknowledgment of God's goodness and provision.

2. Transformation of Heart: Practicing gratitude cultivates humility and a deeper trust in God's providence, strengthening one's spiritual resilience and faith journey.

Practical Ways to Cultivate Gratitude

Gratitude is a transformative practice that can be nurtured through intentional daily habits. Here are effective ways to cultivate gratitude in your life:

1. Keeping a Gratitude Journal:

- ❖ **Purpose:** Dedicate a few minutes each day to write down things you are grateful for. This practice helps shift focus from challenges to blessings.

❖ **Method:** List specific events, people, or moments that brought joy or comfort. Reflect on why these experiences matter to you.

2. Daily Reflection on Blessings:

❖ **Morning Ritual:** Start your day by reflecting on what you are thankful for. Consider aspects of your life such as health, relationships, opportunities, or personal achievements.

❖ **Evening Review:** Before bed, review your day and identify positive moments or acts of kindness received. This reinforces a mindset of gratitude before sleep.

3. Expressing Gratitude to Others:

❖ **Verbal Acknowledgment:** Take opportunities to verbally express appreciation to friends, family, colleagues, or service providers. Acknowledge their contributions or support.

❖ **Written Notes or Messages:** Send thank-you notes or messages of gratitude. This personal gesture can strengthen relationships and uplift others' spirits.

4. Gratitude Walk or Meditation:

❖ **Nature Connection:** Take a walk outdoors and reflect on the beauty of nature around you. Notice details like sunlight, fresh air, or natural scenery, and express gratitude for them.

❖ **Mindful Meditation:** Practice mindfulness by focusing on your breath and silently naming things you are thankful for. This centers your thoughts on gratitude and fosters inner peace.

5. Acts of Service and Kindness:

❖ **Giving Back:** Volunteer or perform acts of kindness for others in need. Serving others cultivates empathy and gratitude for your own blessings.

❖ **Random Acts:** Surprise someone with a small gift, gesture, or supportive message. Spreading positivity can create a ripple effect of gratitude in your community.

6. Gratitude Challenges and Goals:

❖ **Setting Intentions:** Establish gratitude goals, such as finding three things to be thankful for each day. Challenge yourself to notice and appreciate blessings in unexpected moments.

❖ **Accountability:** Share your gratitude journey with a friend or join a gratitude challenge group. Accountability and support can reinforce your commitment to practicing gratitude.

Incorporating these practical strategies into your daily routine can foster a mindset of gratitude, leading to greater emotional resilience, improved relationships, and a deeper sense of contentment in life.

Chapter Eleven

Be Yourself, Love Yourself, Like Yourself

Introduction

God made everyone perfect in His own image! In a world often filled with expectations and pressures to conform, the pursuit of authenticity and self-acceptance stands as a beacon of personal freedom and fulfillment. Embracing who we truly are, without masks or pretenses, is not only liberating but essential to living a meaningful life. It is in this authenticity that we discover our purpose—God's unique design for each of us—and find profound joy in aligning ourselves with His divine plan.

Throughout history and across cultures, individuals who have embraced their authentic selves have often become beacons of inspiration, showing us the beauty and power of living in alignment with our true identities. This chapter explores the journey towards authenticity and self-acceptance, inviting us to uncover our purpose, embrace our uniqueness, and experience the deep joy that comes from walking in God's intended path for our lives.

Purpose and Joy

Every person is uniquely crafted by God, endowed with gifts, talents, and a distinct purpose designed specifically for them. This divine blueprint is not merely a concept but a profound reality that shapes our lives and directs our paths. When we embrace the idea that we have a purpose ordained by God, it transforms the way we view ourselves and our journey through life.

Discovering Your Purpose

Finding one's purpose begins with seeking God and understanding His intentions for our lives. The Bible is filled with stories of individuals who discovered their purpose through their relationship with God. From Moses leading the Israelites out of Egypt to Esther saving her people, these narratives illustrate that purpose is often revealed through faith, obedience, and a willingness to follow God's lead.

When we align our lives with God's purpose, we experience a sense of fulfillment that goes beyond superficial happiness. This purpose is not just about achieving goals or fulfilling dreams; it's about living in a way that honors God and contributes to His kingdom. It's the sweet spot where our passions, talents, and God's call converge, bringing deep-seated joy and contentment.

The Joy of Fulfilling Your Purpose

Living out our purpose brings joy because it connects us to something larger than ourselves. When we are in the center of God's will, we find that our actions, no matter how small, have eternal significance. This realization infuses our lives with a sense of meaning and satisfaction that is unparalleled.

Consider the stories of individuals who have found their purpose and the joy that followed. For instance, when David chose to fight Goliath, he wasn't just defeating a giant; he was stepping into his destiny as a warrior of faith. His courage and faith in God brought him victory and a deep, abiding joy that came from knowing he was fulfilling his purpose.

Similarly, when we step out in faith, trusting God with our lives, we open the door to a life filled with purpose and joy. It is a journey of discovery, where each step taken in faith brings us closer to understanding God's unique plan for us.

In essence, living out our purpose is not just about what we do; it's about who we are becoming in the process. It's a path that leads to a richer, more fulfilling life, grounded in the knowledge that we are exactly who God created us to be, doing exactly what He designed us to do. And in this journey, we find the true essence of joy—a joy that is deep, lasting, and rooted in our relationship with Him.

Laughter and Relationships

Laughter is not just a reaction; it's a vital component of a joyful and fulfilling life. It breaks down barriers, strengthens bonds, and lightens even the heaviest of burdens. Jennifer Bailey wisely advises us to "surround yourself with people of the same sense of humor." This simple yet profound advice underscores the importance of shared laughter in building and nurturing relationships.

The Importance of Laughter

Laughter is a universal language that transcends differences and connects people on a deep level. It releases endorphins, reduces stress, and enhances our overall sense of well-being. In relationships, whether with friends, family, or romantic partners, sharing moments of laughter creates memories and strengthens emotional connections.

Think about the times when laughter has transformed a difficult situation or brought joy to a mundane day. It has the power to uplift spirits, improve communication, and foster a positive atmosphere. When we surround ourselves with people who share our sense of humor, we create an environment where laughter thrives, enriching our lives and relationships.

Being Secure in Yourself

Being secure in oneself is foundational to living a fulfilled life. It means embracing our strengths and weaknesses, accepting who we are, and trusting in our worth. This confidence radiates outward, influencing how we interact with others and how we perceive the world around us.

When we are secure in ourselves, we are less swayed by external opinions and more resilient in the face of challenges. It allows us to pursue our passions, express our beliefs, and form authentic connections with others. This inner security is not about arrogance or perfection but about a deep-seated belief in our inherent value as individuals created by God.

Embracing Self-Assurance

1. Knowing Their Worth: Recognize that their value comes from God, who created them uniquely and with purpose.

2. Setting Boundaries: Establish boundaries that protect their emotional well-being and honor their values and beliefs.

3. Seeking Growth: Continuously learn and grow, embracing opportunities for personal development and spiritual maturity.

When we are secure in ourselves, we are better able to build meaningful relationships, pursue our dreams with confidence, and experience the fullness of joy that comes from living authentically and purposefully. It's a journey of self-discovery and acceptance that leads to a life filled with laughter, love, and deep satisfaction.

Being Secure in Yourself

Being secure in oneself is foundational to living a fulfilled and joyful life. It involves cultivating a deep sense of confidence and acceptance of who you are as an individual. Here's why being secure in yourself is crucial and how it impacts personal happiness:

1. Confidence and Self-Acceptance:

Embrace your strengths and weaknesses. Recognize that each person is unique, with their own talents, quirks, and experiences. Confidence stems from understanding and accepting these aspects of yourself, knowing that they contribute to your individuality and value.

2. Freedom from Comparison:

Secure individuals are less likely to compare themselves to others. They understand that everyone's journey is different and that their worth isn't defined by external achievements or appearances. This freedom from comparison allows them to focus on personal growth and fulfillment.

3. Resilience and Emotional Well-Being:

Self-assurance fosters resilience in the face of challenges and setbacks. When you are secure in yourself, you're better equipped to handle criticism, rejection, or failure without letting it shake your core sense of worth. This resilience promotes emotional well-being and inner peace.

4. Authenticity in Relationships:

Authenticity thrives when you're secure in yourself. You can express your thoughts, feelings, and beliefs genuinely without fear of judgment or rejection. This openness fosters deeper connections and meaningful relationships built on trust and mutual understanding.

5. Pursuit of Goals and Dreams:

Secure individuals are more likely to pursue their goals and dreams with determination. They believe in their abilities and are willing to take risks to achieve their aspirations. This proactive approach to life leads to a sense of accomplishment and fulfillment.

6. Impact on Personal Happiness:

Ultimately, being secure in yourself enhances personal happiness. It allows you to live authentically, pursue meaningful experiences, and find joy in everyday life. When you are confident in who you are, you're able to navigate life's challenges with grace and gratitude, appreciating the journey and celebrating your successes along the way.

Encouraging Self-Assurance:

Encourage readers to cultivate self-assurance by:

- ❖ **Practicing Self-Compassion:** Be kind to yourself and acknowledge your worthiness.
- ❖ **Setting Healthy Boundaries:** Protect your emotional well-being by establishing boundaries in relationships and activities.
- ❖ **Embracing Growth:** Continuously learn and grow, embracing opportunities for personal development and self-discovery.

By fostering a sense of security within themselves, individuals can lead more fulfilling lives, contribute positively to their communities, and experience the profound joy that comes from living authentically and confidently.

Authenticity in Relationships

Authenticity in relationships is foundational for fostering genuine connections and mutual understanding. Here's why embracing authenticity can lead to fulfilling relationships and personal growth:

1. Advocate for Authenticity:

Encourage readers to prioritize authenticity in their relationships. Authenticity involves being true to oneself, expressing genuine thoughts, feelings, and values without pretense or façade. It promotes openness and transparency, creating a space where individuals can truly connect on a deeper level.

2. Benefits of Genuine Connections:

Genuine connections formed through authenticity are based on trust and mutual respect. When both parties feel free to be themselves, they can communicate more effectively, resolve conflicts constructively, and support each other through life's challenges. These relationships are enriching and contribute positively to emotional well-being.

3. Mutual Understanding:

Authenticity fosters mutual understanding by allowing individuals to share their true selves. This openness promotes empathy and compassion, as both parties strive to listen, validate, and support each other's experiences and perspectives. Mutual understanding strengthens bonds and builds a foundation of lasting friendship or partnership.

Living Without Pretense

Living authentically offers a sense of liberation and fulfillment:

1. Freedom from Approval-Seeking:

When individuals embrace their true selves, they no longer rely on external validation or approval. They recognize their intrinsic worth and find fulfillment in self-acceptance rather than seeking validation from others.

2. Embracing Vulnerability:

Authentic living involves embracing vulnerability—the courage to be imperfect and expose one's true feelings and struggles. This vulnerability fosters genuine connections and deepens relationships, as it encourages others to reciprocate openness and honesty.

3. Cultivating Self-Confidence:

Living authentically cultivates self-confidence and resilience. It empowers individuals to navigate life's challenges with authenticity and integrity, knowing they are true to their values and beliefs. This self-assurance strengthens personal growth and enhances overall well-being.

Encouraging Authentic Living:

Encourage readers to embrace authenticity by:

- ❖ **Reflecting on Values:** Take time to identify personal values and align actions with these principles.
- ❖ **Practicing Self-Expression:** Express thoughts, feelings, and opinions authentically in conversations and interactions.

❖ **Building Trust:** Foster trust in relationships by demonstrating honesty, reliability, and authenticity.

By advocating for authenticity in relationships and embracing genuine living, individuals can cultivate meaningful connections, enhance personal well-being, and experience the profound joy of being true to themselves and others.

Career and Authenticity

Authenticity plays a crucial role in career satisfaction and success. Here's why embracing authenticity in career pursuits is essential:

1. Necessity of Authenticity:

Authenticity in career choices ensures alignment between personal values, passions, and professional endeavors. When individuals pursue careers that resonate with their authentic selves, they are more likely to experience fulfillment, motivation, and long-term satisfaction in their work.

2. Pursuing Aligned Paths:

Encourage readers to explore career paths that reflect their true interests, strengths, and values. This alignment enables individuals to leverage their natural talents and passions, leading to greater job satisfaction and productivity.

3. Benefits of Authentic Career Choices:

- ❖ **Job Satisfaction:** When individuals engage in work that aligns with their authentic selves, they derive intrinsic satisfaction from their contributions and achievements.
- ❖ **Motivation and Engagement:** Authentic career choices inspire individuals to remain committed and engaged in their professional roles, fostering creativity and innovation.
- ❖ **Resilience:** Authenticity builds resilience, enabling individuals to navigate challenges and setbacks with integrity and perseverance.

Encouraging Authentic Career Pursuits:

- ❖ **Self-Assessment:** Encourage readers to assess their strengths, interests, and values to identify career paths that align with their authentic selves.
- ❖ **Exploration:** Advocate for exploring diverse career opportunities that offer opportunities for growth and development while staying true to personal values.
- ❖ **Networking:** Suggest building professional networks and seeking mentors who value authenticity and can provide guidance and support in career development.

By embracing authenticity in career pursuits, individuals not only enhance their professional fulfillment but also contribute positively to organizational culture and societal impact. Authenticity empowers individuals to make meaningful contributions aligned with their true passions and values, fostering a fulfilling and purpose-driven career journey.

The Power of Your Smile

You never know the true healing, peace, and joy that your smile can bring to someone. It's not about whether your teeth are perfectly aligned. It's about embracing the beauty that God put within you - your power, your wisdom, your strength, your own natural style and uniqueness that makes you, you. Own it. Love it. Celebrate it. And give the gift of your smile and laughter to others. The world needs it!

Chapter Twelve

—·★·—

Conclusion

Throughout this book, we have explored profound themes that resonate deeply with the human experience: happiness versus joyfulness, the power of words, divine protection, the importance of gratitude, and the liberating embrace of authenticity. Each chapter has offered insights and practical wisdom rooted in biblical truths and personal reflections, aimed at guiding readers toward a more fulfilled and purposeful life.

From understanding the nuances between fleeting happiness and blissful joy to discovering the transformative impact of gratitude and the necessity of speaking life into every situation, this journey has emphasized the importance of spiritual growth, self-awareness, and intentional living. We have seen how God's love and promises provide a steadfast foundation for navigating life's challenges and uncertainties.

Remember - Joy = blissfully content, unmoved, unshaken, still striving for goals but living in general peace with life's journey, with the deep insight and understanding of God' daily direction.

Moreover, the encouragement to be authentic in relationships, careers, and personal endeavors underscores the profound freedom that comes from embracing one's true self. Whether through cultivating a positive mindset, nurturing meaningful connections, or pursuing careers aligned with personal values, this book has empowered readers to live authentically and purposefully.

As we conclude, let us carry forward the lessons learned: to speak words of life, to cultivate gratitude in every circumstance, and to trust in God's provision and protection. May these principles guide us toward a life marked by joy, fulfillment, and a deeper understanding of God's purpose for each of us.

SPECIAL THANKS

With special thanks to all family, friends, colleagues, and mentors who have imparted and spoken life and wisdom into my life. Wishing you all many blessings, great health, joy, peace, and prosperity.

www.ingramcontent.com/pod-product-compliance
Lightning Source LLC
Chambersburg PA
CBHW071754150726
47998CB00005B/1937